A TRIP

TO

British Honduras,

AND TO

SAN PEDRO,

REPUBLIC OF HONDURAS.

BY CHARLES SWETT,

OF WARREN COUNTY, Miss.

PRICE ONE DOLLAR.

NEW ORLEANS,

PRICE CURRENT PRINT, 129 & 131 Gravier St.

1868.

PREFACE.

As we have stated in "Prefatory Remarks" that we were opposed to emigration to Honduras, it may be necessary for us to say that we have, in the following account, given a description of what we saw, faithfully, and as far as possible without prejudice.

It was our intention to publish "Prefatory Remarks" at the time the article was written, (October 7, 1867,) but we reserved it for publication in connection with what we should see in Honduras, which is done without altering a word, or the erasure of a single line.

Warren Co., Miss.,
April, 1868.

CHARLES SWETT.

Prefatory Remarks.

Several friends and relatives entertaining the idea of visiting Belize, (British Honduras), communicated their intentions to me and expressed a wish that I should accompany them, which I could not consent to do; but promised to think of the matter and to give them an answer before their departure, feeling satisfied they had not fully determined to go; but being assured that they would go I at last consented to accompany them, provided nothing should occur to prevent. If they go, it is for the purpose of endeavoring to convince themselves that it is a better country than this, and for the purpose of establishing themselves there if they find the country such as they believe it to be. If I go, it will be for the purpose of gratifying those who desire my company, and with no fixed determination to make it my home, but on the contrary, with every feeling of opposition to that portion of the earth's surface. We at present know but little of Belize, and even I may find sufficient inducement to go to that country; but at present, if asked whether I think it would be better to make the change, would answer with a decided negative. We have every reason to believe that country to be covered with jungle and lagoons, from which, the exhalation of phosphuretted and Carburetted hydrogen gas, consequent upon the decomposition of animal and vegetable matter, must be so great as almost to prevent the possibility of strangers escaping its influence, and suffering from a malaria that will produce remittent, intermittent and pernicious fevers. This it is reasonable to expect; and how many of those who must necessarily undergo this acclimation will ever enjoy in future the health which was theirs in our own country?

The latitude is further south and nearer the equator, and it is a well authenticated fact that it is more desirable in a Hygienic point of view to remove from a warm to a cold climate, in a majority of instances, than from a northern to a latitude nearer the equator.

Here most of us are acclimated, and if taken sick we have physicians who are acquainted with the diseases of our section, and our peculiar idiosyncracies, and consequently there would be a better chance of our recovery than would be the case in another latitude, however skillful the treatment of our case might be, if unaccompanied by the circumstances above named. Here we have friends who will rejoice with us in our prosperity, and who will sympathize with us in our misfortunes, which we can not expect in a strange land. In a word, this is home; a land that is ours; doubly ours; having been bequeathed to us by our forefathers, who sacrificed their lives in the war of the revolution, and by those who so recently died in the vain attempt to place our section in a position of independence. Should this country not be dearer than ever to us because of these reflections? Should we not remain here and keep forever green the graves of departed heroes, or should we desert a land that has been bought at such a price, and forget the suffering and privation of those who are now beyond reach of our sympathy, and whom no word of encouragement can reach, but whose memories we should cherish, and whose deeds we should keep forever fresh in our memories? Should we forget the midnight bivouac and scanty meal, with the cold wet ground for our bed and the canopy of heaven our only covering? the long and tiresome marches, through rain, snow and ice, with naked feet and ragged clothing? Should we banish the recollection of all this from our minds, and leave blank the place now occupied by such hallowed memories? No, let us deliberate well before we leave our homes. It is a serious matter at any time, and particularly so at the present. It is a step that should not be taken without the most careful and exhaustive consideration, and until we are satisfied the change will be greatly to our advantage. Immediately after the close of the war, a distinguished confederate general, in a letter to myself, stated it to be his determination to go to Mexico should it be necessary for him to leave here, yet at the same time stated it to be his determination to remain here as long as he could, and said he would advise all to do so as long as it could be done with honor and safety.

At the time of receiving this letter I contemplated going to Mexico, but the whole current of my thoughts was changed, and I almost came to the positive conclusion to remain here as long as it could be done with "honor and safety." Since then, events have rapidly transpired which have been of a character to almost justify a determination to change, yet such was not my feeling at the time the contemplated trip was made known to me, nor is it at present; though, under a certain condition of things, any land might possibly be better than our own, which condition has not yet arrived, and I sincerely hope it may never be our misfortune to witness. Since the late war, thousands have left this country with the view to bettering their condition, and many more contemplate leaving, notwithstanding the fact that few, if any, of all who made the change have been able to render such an account of their new homes as to induce their friends to follow. Many have gone, and more will go without giving the subject the consideration it demands, but make the leap in the dark, and without calculating the result if they fail to leap the chasm, and should reach the bottom of an unfathomable abyss of future misery, want and suffering. We have from time to time been visited by so called agents of foreign and more favored lands (?) who, in too many instances care very little what ultimately becomes of their dupes so long as their own coffers are filled, and who have studied the most attractive means to remove any objection to the section they pretend to represent that may be raised by those who are opposed to emigrating. They represent to the lazy and indolent that, by emigrating to their chosen spot they will find a country so favored by nature, and in which the spontaneous productions of the soil are so varied and bountiful, as to preclude the necessity of labor, and to the more grasping and avaricious they represent that a fortune is in store for them, and when acquired they will be enabled to successfully establish themselves where they please. These two classes of persons are of little, if any, use anywhere, and can be very well spared from our own "Sunny South"; but there is another class that is being induced to leave us, who will, if they remain, contribute largely by their energy and industry in doing all that can be done towards re-establishing us in a condition of independence, and to a great extent recuperate our now shattered fortunes. It is this latter portion of our people that we desire should remain, and not be led astray by the "wolf in sheep's clothing." It cannot be questioned that at this time the whole country is in a condition of greater pecuniary prostration than we have ever before realized, and that our section seems to have reached so low a point as almost to have passed the limit that will justify the hope of recuperation; yet we are satisfied "when things get to their worst they generally improve," and in this reflection there is room for a little hope, if not for great buoyancy of spirits. It is to be regretted that the time of improvement in our circumstances is in the dim and distant future; so far, indeed, that we are unable to penetrate the gloom by which we are surrounded, and through which there is scarcely a gleam of light to direct us on our way. The work of a people in recuperating their condition after such losses as we have sustained, in a financial point of view only, must necessarily be slow, and require time for its consummation ; but with us it can safely be said there is no foundation on which to build, or at least it is of such a character as to prevent our rearing a superstructure that will promise durability and satisfaction. We are deprived of our former labor system, that enabled us to increase our wordly possessions and enrich the North, and are now compelled to depend upon a system of labor that prevents the possibility of our raising our great staple productions at a price that will prove remunerating. Our cotton, that at one time enabled us to contribute so much towards defraying the expenses of the Government, can do so no longer, and those who have been engaged in its cultivation since the war, must discontinue it, as loss has attended nearly every effort to produce it by our own people who were acquainted with the plant, and a like want of success has attended the trials made by those who have come from other sections, and who knew but little of its cultivation, and whose capital was the only advantage they possessed over us. Again, it is well known that Europe no longer looks to this country for its supply of cotton, and that we have lost control of the cotton markets of the world, which was not the case before the war. We are without capital, and very few are willing to invest their means in our section during the present disturbed condition of our affairs.

The destruction of our great planting interests has reduced

us to a consuming, instead of being, as formerly, a producing people, and we cannot expect for a long time to come that we will occupy any other position. The history of the world produces sufficient evidence by the experience of all who have gone before us, that a people to be prosperous must have the balance of trade in their favor, or at least there should not be such a difference as at present exists between ourselves and the rest of the world. If we cannot raise the staples it was formerly our custom to produce in such quantity, and at such price as to enable us to govern the markets that required them for consumption, it may be well to ask what we can raise. There can be no doubt of our ability to produce all, or nearly all we may require to subsist upon, but what can we raise for export, and thereby prevent the excessive balance of trade being against us that we know to have been the case during the past three years? The question is more easily asked than answered. The successful cultivation of the soil will insure prosperity in every business and pursuit, and a failure will produce a corresponding or proportionate depression in every occupation the human family is engaged in. Although we have a climate as genial as any on earth, and a soil as rich, we must come to the unfortunate conclusion that our agricultural pursuits must languish for a time, and during that time we must remain a consuming people, and consequently be poorer to-day than we were yesterday. For every evil there is a remedy, if we only knew how and when to apply it, and all who read these pages are as capable of applying it as myself, and it is hoped, more so****** These thoughts are suggested by the fact of our having been almost entirely engaged in planting, and but comparatively little in manufacturing, and show plainly how poor we have become as a people. This condition causes many to look about them to endeavor to fix upon some spot where they may have a more favorable prospect of making a living than at present seems to be the case here. The primary cause of the dissatisfaction of our people, and the cause of every evil we are now subjected to is, the political atmosphere of the country, and no apparent prospect of its changing for the better at an early day. We are politically nothing—taxed beyond precedent—denied representation—almost deprived of the ability to pay taxes, and without a voice in the formation of those laws by which we are to be governed—the party in power striving by every means in its power to place an inferior race in a position of political importance, and to even elevate to social equality a people it was undoubtedly the intention of our Creator should occupy a position below us, and be under our direction as certainly as it was His intention that the superior should control the inferior. This is a gloomy array of evils, and should it not rather cause us to buckle on our armor and to make a powerful effort to keep this country under the control of white men? There are thousands of our friends who must permanently abide here, come weal or come woe; and should we not feel it incumbent upon us to remain and engage in that political contest for supremacy which must eome sooner or later, and prehaps at an early day? a struggle that will be more fiercely contested than any we have gone through when the sullen boom of artillery, the rattle of musketry, and the dying groans of our friends and relatives were heard—a contest fraught with more momentous issues than it has ever been the duty of a nation before to engage in, as it will settle the question whether we are to be slaves or freemen—whether we are to be governed by intelligence, or by an ignorant population, whose principal idea of liberty seems to be that it consists in the removal of every restraint, the absence of all law. Let us make a determined effort to save the old ship that has weathered so many storms, and is now in the breakers, aud in danger of being dashed in pieces, and not say we care not who is at the helm, or how fiercely the storm rages. If, after using every means at our command, the vessel is wrecked, we may then seize a plank and trust to the Giver of all Good to waft us to a harbor of safety.

What have we yet done to check the current that seems hurrying us to destruction? Nothing, simply nothing; and the idea that we are too weak, is too feeble an argument for men to use who have undergone what we have from 1861 to the present time. What we have done since the close of the war has encouraged the radical party to make greater demands than they would have thought of making, bnt for our concessions from time to time.

We have taken counsel from our fears, and have done too much through policy, a fruit that has a most inviting exterior, but within is bitter indeed. Let us in future claim all we feel we are entitled to, and contend for it with all our power; again I say let us do our duty, and if we are overtaken and overpowered, let every true and honored southron be prepared to exclaim, "Shake not thy gory locks at me; thou can'st not say I did it," and let him gather together the fragments he may have saved from the wreck, leave the home of his childhood, the graves of his kindred, and seek some land where he may have the satisfaction of rearing his children in the midst of those who have feelings in common with them, and with whom they may associate on terms of equality. We have sacrificed nearly our entire property in the vain endeavor to better our condition; and let us show to the world our willingness to make other and greater sacrifices, but not to the end that radicalism shall rule this land—the fairest of earth, and surrender to those who are in every way unfitted to occupy it, the heritage of our fathers.

No, rather than this should be, better, far better that this land should sink, and that waves of ocean should roll over what was once a happy and a prosperous country—that the map of the world should show no spot once occupied by our territory—our names be a myth—our requiem be the howling winds and the roaring waves, and our dirge the scream of the gull in his passage over our ruined homes and unknown graves. Better, far better that all save honor and the immortal soul should be lost, than that party whose motto seems to be equality, in every sense in which it can be used, should prevail. We can accomplish something, and let us do what we can; and if we fail, we will have the proud consolation of knowing we made every effort to keep our country in the enviable position it has hitherto occupied among the nations of the earth. If despite our exertions to the contrary, our country should be brought to the humiliating fact of equality of races existing among us—when an inferior holds public position, and even serve in the capacity of representatives of the people, or when we are satisfied this will be the result of what is now transpiring, it will be well to surrender this land to our persecutors, and time will make known whether they have acted well or wisely. Let each and every one do what seemeth unto him best, keeping in view the fact that there is still a duty for all to perform, and which should be accomplished, if possible, regardless of what the consequences may be. We have work to do not for ourselves only, but for generations yet unborn, and who will hardly think of us with veneration if we fail to exert ourselves in this crisis in a manner commensurate with the importance of the questions involved. It may be too late to accomplish good, but it can never be too late to make the attempt.

Under certain circumstances it will be seen I favor emigration and this may be the most favorable time for such a movement. At all events, I shall, on my return from Belize, publish all the information gathered in that country, and if it serves as a guide to even one in the formation of an opinion as to what is best to be done, some little good may be accomplished.

It is my intention to get information from the most reliable sources, and to describe as nearly as possible what is seen, and as the trip is not for purposes of speculation, I hope to be able to give a correct, though condensed account of that distant land in every particular that promises to be of profit to those who contemplate making it their future residence. * * * * * * *

This is the land of my birth and where I had hoped to be able to live in the peaceful enjoyment of my own. It has been my desire here to be buried, and that my ashes might mingle with those of my kindred, but it may be otherwise ordained, and be my lot to repose in a land far distant from the scenes of my childhood; and if so, I will cast the anchor of hope in such waters as my destiny may waft me to, ever trusting in Him who "doeth all things well," to carry me safely through my earthly pilgrimage and finally to a haven of eternal rest.

Warren Co., Miss., October 7th, 1867.

DIARY.

DECEMBER 26tb.—Our party, according to agreement, left "Old Warren" this morning by rail for Belize, via New Orleans, though two of our number remain behind and will follow by the next steamer, if we do not give such a representation on our arrival at our point of destination, as to make it unnecessary for them to come, as we can write by return of steamer, being informed she lies at Belize several days. We reached New Orleans in safety, at 8 A. M., and are now located at the St. Charles. Never before have I had such feelings as possess me at this time I know not how to express them. It is certainly nothing new for me to be absent from home, the late war having necessitated that from its beginning to its end, with the exception of a few days; but this trip oppresses me with feelings of sadness. What am I about to do? To leave my native land, it is hoped, for a short time, but to engage in a tour of observation for the benefit, I trust, of many, but not with the desire or intention to influence any. Not having inaugurated this expedition, as stated in my prefatory remarks, and representing others, it is my earnest wish to give a clear and unvarnished statement of all I see, and all that is heard from reliable sources, ever preferring an occular demonstration, when possible, to representations of any one, not because of a want of confidence in my fellow man, or fear of being deceived, feeling satisfied that such letters as we carry will place us properly before the officials, but because such information can not fail to be of a more gratifying character to those who desire facts, intermingled with no portion of fiction.

2

In the morning our party will proceed to get together such articles as we may need for the trip, not trusting to our getting anything at Belize.

DECEMBER 27th.—To-day was spent in completing our outfit, and in obtaining letters, in which latter undertaking we were very much assisted by General B., who secured for us an introduction to the British Consul, and a letter from him direct to his Excellency the Governor of Honduras.

DECEMBER 28th.—Not having quite completed our arrangements on yesterday, we are making a finish to-day, and must be on shipboard by 5 P. M., according to advertisement, though there is no absolute necessity for hurry on that account, as they are known not to be quite as punctual as the sun. Our purchases being completed, and on board at 4 o'clock, we left the hotel for the steamer Trade-Wind, expecting to be in the gulf before morning. The vessel was ready to sail by 7 o'clock, but a dense fog rising, we lay at the pier all night, much to our disappointment, as we are anxious to get forward as rapidly as possible, but we must accept the situation as additional evidence of the fallibility of human calculation, which we can safely do without fear of being opposed by this cloud of vapor for any length of time. Would we could say as much of that cloud which obscures in its sable folds our political horizon, and now seems threatening to veil the star of hope with its funereal pall; the first produces not a disagreeable sensation of chilliness, but the latter penetrating the inmost recesses of the heart and causing a degree of cold that cannot be removed by any ordinary means.

DECEMBER 29th.—This morning we find ourselves still at the pier, but not without hope of being able to get off in an hour or two. The fog disappearing at 7.45 A. M., we left our moorings and may now consider ourselves on our way. This being Sunday, we had Divine Service; the Rev. Mr. Morrill, of Texas, preaching, who, although over sixty years of age, is on his way to a new country, and though in feeble health, does not fear to brave any hardship he may have to encounter, or any privation he may be called upon to suffer. In the evening we had a discourse from the Rev. Mr. Pearce, of Mississippi, who is on board with his family, and goes for the purpose of locating, though he has never seen the country. His faith and determination cannot but be admired, though I confess that it would require more than the writer ever had or ever expects to possess, to induce a move of the same kind. It is perhaps best that the Pioneer should sever every connection with his former home, and then, if dissatisfied with a new country at first, he will remain and eventually become reconciled to those customs and things that at first made an unfavorable impression, and might have induced a departure from a land that promised less than was expected. To-day has been gloomy, with rain, which increased as the day advanced, and as we come to anchor, just inside the bar, there is every appearance of a storm. Here we must lay till morning; it being impossible to go over the bar to-night.

Our careful commander informs us it is possible we may have to remain at our anchorage for several hours in the morning.

December 30th.—This morning it is cloudy, cool and windy, and our captain has determined to remain till the middle of the day, if the weather does not sooner improve; he represents the outside to be pretty rough, with the wind in its present direction. There are many on board who would prefer smooth water, and though they were anxious to leave the Crescent City, and have shown some impatience at each delay, are now willing to abide by the decision of one who has the reputation of being an excellent seaman; all fearing sea-sickness, which is anything but agreeable, those who have experienced its effects state that when under its influence, is the best possible time for a man to take his departure to the land of spirits, and a person suffering from it will not unfrequently request to be rolled overboard, with the view of trying the water-cure. We trust our knowledge of it may be confined to what we have heard, not feeling anxious to verify those statements. By the way, we have been told by the initiated, it is not a bad plan to take a little spirits to prevent nausea. Not having tried it, can say nothing of its efficacy, but we can all add our testimony to the fact that the prescription is not a bad one, and having a supply of the medicine with us, it is not improbable we may try it. We have also been informed that champagne is very good for the same purpose, but as our finances are not in as healthy a condition as in former days, as "Bill Arp" said, when asked what state he lived in, " The less we say about that the better."

At 11 o'clock, the wind having died away, and our pilot being on board, we weighed anchor and again pursued our way to the South-West pass, through which we make our entrance to the Gulf. We found a heavy sea outside, which soon caused sea-sickness with most of those who were for the first time being tossed upon the "briny deep." The writer was one of the first to succumb, notwithstanding the remedy above spoken of, and the most powerful exercise of the will in connection. There was no wish for the table during that day or the next, or the next, and the dinner bell was even resorted to with no effect. It is perhaps well enough to state here, that those who contemplate making a sea voyage for the first time should be thoroughly impressed with the fact that they are about to leave home, and home comforts, and shou'd prepare themselves in every way possible to meet the exigencies that may arise, and not trust to obtaining them on shipboard, as those who have control of vessels are acted upon by the same influences that control persons in other situations in life, and feel that to provide for themselves is the first step, and, perhaps, with too many the last that should be taken. Let all be provided with such simple medicines as they are in the habit of using at home, with lemons, or sugar of lemon, which is very convenient, spoons, mugs, crushed sugar, ale or porter, and a small quantity of such liquors and wine as they may prefer ; feeling satisfied that by such means much suffering will be prevented : and even should the articles not be used and it should be necessary to throw them away, the loss can not be great. Five gallons of water and, if possible, some ice, would not be out of place in a voyage from New Orleans to Belize.

December 31st.—The weather is cloudy, and with a good breeze and steam, we are making very good headway, and we earnestly hope to make a quick trip. Very few persons are able to be about, nearly all being confined to their berths. We have over one hundred passengers on board, with quite a number of ladies and children among them, and when mother and child are both sick, the poor little one sadly feels the loss of the parent's seothing influences.

January 1.—We are still tossed upon the waves and very few are in condition to eat a New Year's dinner, if within reach, but nothing is heard of any such preparation. For a time, though we are to be separated from our homes, and to be surrounded by a waste of waters, which we may not inappropriately consider emblematic of the present condition of our unfortunate and oppressed South, which seems separate from the world, and to occupy no political position, and which is lashed by angry political waters which threaten the destruction of the old Ship of State, we are united in our determination to carve out for our friends and selves some plan by which we may have a voice in the "laws by which we are governed," though of course we cannot expect to act in that direction any further than to give evidence of what will promote our welfare, and trust to the kindness of those in whose midst we may be, to feel and to exercise sufficient charity towards us, to cause them, in some measure, to provide for our political wants.

January 2.—We find in our little vessel many gentlemen from Louisiana, Arkansas, Mississippi and from other Southern States, who, before the war were in affluent circumstances, and consequently removed from the necessity of performing any kind of manual labor, now express their willingness to do, as far as they are able, whatever may be necessary to enable them to make a support for themselves and families. We have a most excellent list of passengers, and have been very fortunate in forming a party for exploration, consisting of some of the best men it has ever been our fortune to meet with. All seem firmly impressed with the necessity for a change, and the determination they evince, and the willingness they express to combat any hardship they may have to encounter, and to overcome all obstacles that may be presented, is a pretty good evidence that success is likely to attend their efforts, or at least affords us reasonable hope that such will be the final result.

January 3.—The weather still continues somewhat cloudy, which is fortnnate for us, as the temperature is lower in consequence, though we have at no time since leaving New Orleans found it as high as in that city. Indeed, though we are approaching the equator, the remarkable fact has impressed all, that the heat is less oppressive from day to day. To-morrow we should be at Belize, but the prospect now is that we will not reach our destination before the next day. Patience is a virtue, but all are extremely anxious to get where more freedom of locomotion may be enjoyed.

JANUARY 4.—To-day the hitherto unbroken and monotonous blank has been broken by the appearance of land, and all are cheered by the sight, and now feel satisfied this is the last day of our voyage, which has already extended to a greater length than any of us could have wished. Before leaving our homes, we were informed the trip would occupy four days; by the time we reach New Orleans, five days, which by the time we reached the mouth of the river had extended to six, and our unfortunate experience is that seven are required; at least such has been the time on our passage, we having cast anchor this evening, at about 6 o'clock, off the town of Belize, British Honduras, and step number one may now fairly be considered terminated.

Before leaving the scene I feel it to be my duty to speak in terms of praise of our purser, Col. Harney, who is an ex-confederate, and a whole-souled, liberal gentleman; and of Mr. Scoville, chief engineer of the boat, through whose kindness we were supplied with one of the best rooms on the vessel, he having with a spirit of liberality and self denial rarely witnessed in these days of selfishness, resigned to our use his own room, thereby subjecting himself to inconvenience, but we sincerely hope, not to discomfort. May he never feel the want of a friend, and may his pilgrimage through life be attended with as few obstructions as fall to the lot of man. We will ever hold him in grateful remembrance. We are all anxious to get ashore to-night, but having made earnest efforts to do so, and failing, must rest content till morning. One thing is consoling, however, we are in smooth water, compared with what we have passed over, and the vessel being still, have the prospect of a good nights's rest, which will be worth something to us, and indeed is much needed by all.

JANUARY 5.—We succeeeded in getting ashore this morning by 9 o'clock, and finding no hotel for our accommodation, fortunately made arrangements with Mr. Mahler, an old resident of the place, to provide for our wants, which he did during our stay here, in good style; taking the house formerly occupied for the same purpose by Mr. Ware. From this location we have a beautiful view of the Bay, and have nothing in front to obstruct the breeze, which is truly delightful.

JANUARY 6—To-day we have an opportunity of looking around us, and must say our impressions of Belize, from report, have been very different from the reality.

We find a very well built town of about 7000 inhabitants, and doing a very considerable business. The houses are mostly one story, but we will give hereafter a full description of the place and its surroundings. We to-day formed a party for purposes of exploration, consisting of the following gentlemen, who were passengers on the Trade Wind:

Rev. Levi Pearce..........of Sharon, Mississippi.
Col. J. F. Harrison........of Tensas, Louisiana.
Danl. Swett...............of Vicksburg, Miss.
Dr. G. P, Frierson.........of DeSoto, Louisiana.
Dr. G. A. Frierson......... " "
Dr. R. F. Gray ....of Opelousas, "
Capt. W. Buckner.........of Tensas, "
J. S. Peak................of Chicot, Arkansas.
E. V. Frierson ....of DeSoto, Louisiana.

T. C. Frierson .... " "
T. F. Owen .... of Catahoula, "
Thos. P. Kane .... of Jackson, "
T. P. Morris .... of Batesville, Arkansas.
Chas. Swett .... of Warren Co., Miss.

and last, though not an unimportant personage, Wm. Owens, an "American citizen of African descent," who accompanies Col. H. to serve him in the capacity of cook, being an old servant of the Colonel. We to-day visited Mr. Jas. M. Putnam, formerly of the U. S., and who is at present acting as agent for the firm of Messrs. Young, Toledo & Co., of Belize, in the sale of their lands, and through his kindness received an introduction to Messrs. McDonald and Harrison, who are in charge of the business of the firm at this place. Our interview was very pleasant, and we found these gentlemen ready to grant every facility in their power to enable us to carry to a successful issue, the objects of our mission. We were also introduced by Mr. P. to Mr. Mathe, with whom we spent a very pleasant hour in the evening, and obtained from him some very interesting facts connected with his experience as a sugar planter, which we regret to say has thus far not proved very profitable.

January 7th.—Having letters to Gov. Longdon, we called upon his excellency to-day, being accompanied by Mr. P., and were very kindly received. While we were not discouraged by the interview, we can say that Gov. Longdon did not at once accept as fact the many reports concerning the great agricultural and planting properties of the Colony, but gave us every reason to believe that what could be done by the government, in conformity with its laws, to promote the welfare of emigrants, would be done, but at the same time would offer no extraordinary inducements to emigrants. Some of our party believing that they could become British Subjects, in its most extended sense, were informed by his excellency, that after they had selected the country as their place of residence, should they make application for letters of naturalization, they would be granted, but they would only entitle the recipient to colonial protection, while in the colony, and not to the protection of the British Government when removed beyond the limits of the Colony. Some were much disappointed at this, as they had hoped by becoming citizens they would secure to themselves the guardian care of certainly the best government on earth, wherever they might be, so long as they claimed their home in British Honduras.

JANUARY 8th.—Being busy to-day in completing our preparations to explore the bush, we again called in requisition the aid of our friend, Mr. Putnam, who is ever ready to assist all who visit Honduras to an extent that has, and will continue to trespass heavily upon his time, though he seems able to, or at least does, the work of about three men. Having deemed it best to do so, have secured a schooner, by charter, to convey us to any point we may desire to visit, and for an indefinite length of time. Our party being divided into committees, in order to facilicitate business, we hope to be off to-morrow. Since our arrival here, the breeze has been constantly blowing very freshly from the bay, and at night we were lulled to sleep by its sighing through the lattice, the sound would alternately rise to Eolian sweetness, and almost die away, which was peculiarly grateful to the feelings, and far from being unpleasant to the ear; but what pleasure was ever unalloyed, or continued for any length of time without interruption? The wind entirely died away at 8 o'clock this evening, and before ten changed to the north-west, causing an invasion of our premises by such a force of *sand flies* as to render opposition futile, and we were punished to a degree that it is impossible for us to make known, but will ever be remembered; being entirely without bars, except the writer, who was supplied with one made this morning, of muslin, but at the moment out of reach because needed. Suffice it to say for the present that, they gave no notice of their approach, came in immense force, and each individual armed with what seemed to us to be a red-hot needle, which they used with a vigor worthy of a better cause, and served to admonish the poor "ex-confeds" that it was still their destiny to suffer.

January 9th.—This morning the wind is blowing from the opposite direction, sand flies are gone, and we will endeavor to forget the miseries of the past night, and more particularly, as we have determined not to be checked by any obstacle or annoyance we may meet with, but to battle cheerfully every opposing cause in striving for the end we wish to attain. Although we had fully expected to make a start this morning, the very disagreeable information is imparted to us that the vessel chartered yesterday can not go, and we are under the necessity of getting another. Fortunately, a schooner is in port from Omoa, which we have engaged, and which is now unloading, therefore can reasonably expect to leave Belize in the distance to-morrow, at furthest. It would have been better had we visited the schooner before chartering her, but we did not, yet feel it our duty to make the following statement, in the hope it may be of some service to those who may hereafter be situated as we were. Between Omoa and Belize a considerable trade is carried on in swine, by means of schooners varying in capacity from ten to fifty tons, the animals being placed in the hold of the vessel. The schooner selected by us had just arrived with a cargo of this description, and though an attempt was made at cleansing, it became very apparent in the course of a day that the process might have been carried to much greater extent, with decided advantage.

JANUARY 10th.—At 9 this morning we started for the schooner "Three Sisters," of 11 tons, Capt. Francisco Solaro, which was anchored about half a mile from shore, though the Captain and crew did not come aboard till 2.45, P. M., when we weighed anchor for Manatee Bar, eighteen miles distant, and a little west of south from Belize. The pilot who was to accompany us, came on board with the Captain, but without his knowing it returned in the boat that brought them off. After sailing a mile, we came to anchor, and Capt. Solaro returned to Belize to investigate the conduct of the pilot. Being pleasantly located, and a delightful breeze blowing from the north-west, must exercise patience, our stock of which we did not find excessive, as requisition has to be made in that direction very frequently, for very large quantities, to be delivered in the very best order, and immediately. At 3.45 the Captain returned without the pilot, and we again weighed anchor and proceeded on our way without that individual, although we feel the necessity of having one, as our captain does not know all the points we desire to visit. Having heard much of Spanish Honduras during our few days stay at Belize, several of our party desire to visit that country, whatever may be the result of our present trip, as it will occupy but a few days to do so, and we can then verify or disprove by occular demonstration the extravagant stories we have heard of the Republic. Thermometer, F. 6 A. M., 72; 12 M., 82½; 6 P. M., 82½.

JANUARY 11th.—Finding that we could not reach Manatee

Bar before night, in consequence of our late start, have concluded to go on, and visit it on our return. At a reasonable hour at night we disposed ourselves for sleep; the older gentlemen occupying the four berths of the cabin, others taking the hold of the vessel, and some using their hammocks, slung in the rigging: ourself and one other taking the top of the cabin, which was elevated a few feet above deck. At 12½ all on deck were aroused by a shower, delivered by a passing cloud, and which cooled the atmosphere to such an extent as to make two blankets decidedly comfortable, and of course one each was the extent of our supply in that direction. As for the wetting we received, our experience in that way has been too extensive in time past to give it a passing thought. It being so very cool we examined the thermometer and to our astonishment found it to indicate 83°., although these is no breeze, and our vessel is drifting with the current. This remarkable difference between actual, and from one's feelings, apparent temperature, we will revert to again when on the subject of climate.

JANUARY 11th.—At 6 A. M. we were very near the mouth of North Stann Creek, distant thirty-five miles from Belize, and made for it in order to go ashore. At 7 we cast anchor, and visited a Carib village located here, which we found to extend along the coast for the distance of half a mile, and to contain about 800 inhabitants, and a methodist and a catholic church. Mr. Brown, the police officer of the place, was absent, as was also the methodist minister; therefore, we passed through the village and trusted to our observation for information. We found the houses to be built about square, eighteen feet the usual size, and to be constructed of studding, with cane of the country secured across them, and filled with clay; the roof being very steep, forming an equilateral triangle, and being covered with the split branches of the Cahoon palm. They have no chimneys, no windows with glass, nor floors, except those made of "mother earth." We here saw the manner in which the Cassava root is prepared for bread. (See description of that root.) The root is grated and placed in a long tube, or bag, five feet in length and four inches in diameter, which is suspended from a beam till all sap of the root is drained from it, when it is sifted, made into cakes which are two feet in diameter, and one fourth of an inch thick, and baked. This is called Cassava or pilot bread, and will keep a very long time ; has a cream color, but though we have eaten much of it, do not think we would prefer it, under any circunstances, to the wheaten loaf or the corn cake of our country. Their graters and sifters we deem worthy of description, and are made as follows. The grater is a piece of mahogany 1½ inches thick, 18 inches wide and 2½ feet long, across which lines are drawn three-fourths of an inch apart, which lines are divided along their length so that the division lines will run diagonally, and at each point of division a hole is punched and a pice of broken pebble driven in that will not be more than half the size of a pea, and the grater is complete. The sifter is 3 feet in diameter, and is made of split cane, through which the Cassava is rubbled by the hands, and not by shaking as with us. From eight to ten miles in rear of this place, though the distance does not appear so great, there is a range of high hills. The natives plant at and near the base of these, and depend upon the Belize market for the sale of all they have to dispose of. The coast is not more than two feet above the level of the sea, the waters of which are well stocked with fish, if we can rely upon the statements of the natives.

We also saw quite a quantity of fish drying across poles We here found a dory, made of Spanish cedar, which measure

36 feet in length, 7 feet wide, 3 feet deep, 1½ inches thick and elegantly modeled. After purchasing some oranges at 75 cents per hundred, we returned to the vessel and at 9.20 A. M. weighed anchor for "All Pines," forty-five miles distant from Belize. The natives of the village just left were found to be polite, and willingly answered any questions we propounded, though they frequently manifested some surprise at our ignorance of their manners and customs, and would laugh heartily at our description of the customs of our own country, and the differences that existed among us. They could all speak English, and we therefore had no difficulty in making ourselves understood. Cocoa nuts, oil from the cocoa nut, and oranges was all they offered for sale.

On being asked why the oil was so white and thick, they replied, "it is because the weather is so cold!" The thermometer at the time ranging as high as 76°. There being very little breeze, we did not reach "All Pines" till 2.25 P. M., where we immediately went ashore for the purpose of visiting one of the sugar estates of Mr. Mathé. We found Mr. Debraam, whose residence is on the coast, immediately on landing, who received us very cordially, and expressed his regret that he could not furnish us with conveyance to the estate, three miles distant, that evening, there being too many of us to accommodate thus far, on the limited notice given him, and as we were anxious to keep moving, at once proceeded on foot for the "Estate." For one-half the distance from the coast to the "Estate" we found the country at the time it was opened to have been covered with pine, most of which had been made into lumber and sent to the West Indies by Mr. Debraam. There is quite a large store near the coast, a very complete lumber mill, and a foundry, the property of the Estate. Over the distance between these two points is a most excellent road, which, for about half the way has been thrown up, at great expense, in order to avoid the mud of the wet season. The Estates, there being three in number, and not very far apart, Mr. Debraam superintends the whole, which are situated on the "Sittee" river, and twelve miles from the coast by water though only three by land.

On our way up we saw many cattle, though they did not look so well as we had reason to expect in this land of perpetual pasturage. Mr. Aquet, Mr. Savage and Mr. Hanson, who are in charge of different duties on the premises, very kindly gave us all the information we desired. What we here witnessed would certainly astonish a Louisiana sugar planter. The places were opened in 1863, and Mr. Debraam informed us he expected to make six thousand pounds of sugar per acre, and there being four hundred acres in cultivation, it is a question for the juveniles to decide how much coffee it will sweeten. A gentleman of our party who is well acquainted with the production of sugar, when told of the expectation as to yield, looked incredulous, but after making an examination of the growing crop, remarked that he was prepared to believe ten thousand pounds could be made to the acre if the yield should prove in proportion to the quantity of cane produced, taking the Louisiana yield as his basis. Plenty of the canes were two and a half inches in diameter and fifteen to twenty feet in length. The fields were a perfect mass of vegetation, the canes growing to a certain height, and under their own weight falling over and again growing up, forming curves not unlike the letter S when in this position ∽. Many of us were at first disappointed because of the cane not growing higher, and one of our party caught hold of a top which was not more than three feet above the ground, and asked one of the gentlemen in charge of the place if he called that sugar cane; at the same time giving it a jerk, when it developed the fact that three feet was not its length, but eighteen, which proved satisfactory to all parties concerned. The buildings on the place are not constructed of brick, and might be more properly called sheds, though constructed in the most substantial manner, with galvanized corrugated iron roofing, and the machinery of the most costly and approved patterns. A very large sum has been expended, and thus far no return for the outlay of capital. No plows are used in preparing the ground, but holes are dug with a hoe or machete, in rows six feet apart and three feet in the drill, where the cane is planted in pieces from eight inches to one foot in length, and when once planted it is said to rattoon for fifteen years, and has been known to do so for a greater length of time. The best time for planting the cane is in October and November, though it may be planted at any time during the rainy season—which is said to begin about the first of June and to continue to the end of the year.

The grinding is commenced in from twelve to fourteen months, notwithstanding the statements that have appeared in print that two and three crops can be made in a year. Having made use of the word "Machete" for the first time, and its being an indispensable article in this country, it is as well to describe it here as elsewhere. (It is a heavy knife, from eighteen to twenty-four inches in length, and from two to two and a half inches in width, with a proportionate thickness, and is to the native, his axe, his hatchet, his saw, his plow, harrow, shovel, spade, hoe, pruning knife and weapon of defense. They never go to the woods without it, and we have seen them cut asunder logs eight and ten inches in diameter with them, though of course the implement would have been broken in the hand of one of less experience.) We measured at "All Pines" a Dorey that is perhaps the largest in Honduras. It is thirty-five feet long, eight feet wide and four feet deep, and is to receive machinery that will weigh two tuns, and be used between this point and Belize for the benefit of the "Estates." (See article on Boats).

On reaching the schooner, all were very tired, having walked continually since leaving the vessel, though we have all been amply repaid for the investment of physical exertion, for it can safely be said we have had ocular demonstration of at least one of the wonders of this said to be wonderful portion of the earth. Our next place of landing will be South Stann Creek, fifty miles from Belize, and it being close by, have determined to lay here to-night and make an early start in the morning. Thermometer 6 A. M. 75½; 12 M. 81: 6 P. M. 80½.

JANUARY 12th.—We weighed anchor at 5 A. M., and again cast anchor at South Stann Creek, near the residence of Mr. C. Chamberlin, who has a large body of land at this point, purchased of Mr. Mathé. Mr. C. formerly resided at Natchez, and though he has been in possession of a large property, had his family living within reach of every luxury of life, and is now in possession of a much larger portion of this world's goods than is the case with most of us, this gentleman, with an elegant and accomplished family, reared in luxury, has chosen to lead the life of a pioneer in a comparatively unknown country, where law and order prevail, rather than to remain in a land where there is but little protection, and less prospect of accumulation. May they reap the reward of their determination, enterprise and self denial. Mr. C. having been here for a very short time, has made very little clearing, but having cut a road for ten miles from the coast to the interior, we passed over it under the guidance of Mr. Walker, and found the land very rich, with the Cahoon palm the prevailing growth. For half a mile back from the coast—perhaps not quite so far—it will be necessary to corduroy in order to make a firm road, but beyond this nothing of the kind will be necessary. The ten miles of road terminated at a point on the creek where the bank was fifteen feet high at the time, though the creek was very low—yet there can be no doubt of its being navigable at certain seasons of the year for the "Dorey." We found in our walk a Caoutchouc or India-rubber tree that measured twenty inches in diameter and fifty feet to the first limb. A cut with the Machete caused the sap to flow very freely, and to thicken almost instantly under the action of the atmosphere—a portion of which we scraped off, wrapped in a leaf, and placed among the curiosities in our ever present satchel. The sap, when it exudes from the tree is a light cream color, and the quantity that can be obtained from a tree is almost incredible; the flow being much more rapid than we have ever seen from any other tree. At the landing we found a bamboo that was used as a clothes line, that measured forty-eight feet in length, five inches in diameter at the butt, and two inches in diameter at the other end where it had been cut off, and originally must have been at least sixty feet in length. We also saw an enclosure made with the Pimente, a species of palm growing from twelve to fifteen feet in height and three to four inches in diameter, very straight and without limbs. The fence is made in the following manner: The poles are cut six feet in length, driven into the ground four or six inches, close together, and poles of the same material are placed horizontally within a foot of the top on each side, and opposite, they are then tied with vines, and it is finished. This material is used very extensively throughout the country, for many purposes. Here we also saw some of the native weather-boarding, made from the cabbage or Royal palm tree. This tree has a very straight, smooth body, frequently being fifty feet high, and a foot in diameter. For half an inch of its depth the wood is solid, but the interior is pithy and not unlike the sugar cane in appearance. This tree is felled, and the exterior of the trunk removed in slabs from ten to fourteen feet in length and four to six inches in width. In using it for weather-boarding, one precaution only is necessary—be careful you do not delay the nail driving, for while you can by the use of a Machete bring down a tree a foot in diameter with a few blows, after these boards become dry they are only fit for the wood pile, as they are as hard as horn. The natives will get out these boards for ten dollars per 1000 superficial feet, and furnish their own provision. After enjoying the hospitality of Mr. C. and family during the day, we had a discourse from the Rev. Mr. Pearce, and at a late hour in the afternoon again boarded our water craft, and at 6.15 weighed anchor and set sail for "Seven Hills." We had another rain at mid-night, but the deck is our place, as it is decidedly the most comfortable, rain or shine. The cabin and the hold are now decidedly uncomfortable, for two reasons—the want of breeze, and the absence of pure air; those who have taken up their quarters below, finding it necessary to make frequent and often very lengthy visits to the deck in consequence of the character of the vessel's last cargo. Thermometer 6 A. M., 80; 12 M., 82; 6 P. M., 81.

JANUARY 13.—At 11 A. M., being opposite the mouth of the Rio Grande, 80 miles from Belize, and six miles from shore, in a perfect calm, Dr. G. A. Frierson and myself took the vessel's "Dorey" and two boys of the crew to go ashore for the purpose of getting guides and pitpans (see boats) of Mr. Bennett, manager of the Seven Hills sugar Estate of Messrs. Young Toledo & Co., to whom our party brought letters from the firm at Belize, for the purpose. We landed on an island near the mouth of the river, after having paddled apparently over twice the distance it at first seemed we had to go, and though we found a large native house here, several smaller ones, and three Pitpans, thirty feet in length, concluded to await the arrival of a sail boat three miles north-east of us, and which we hope is coming to the river, before acting farther. Between the schooner and the shore we crossed a shoal that was very thickly strewn with the conch and star-fish, and made several attempts to obtain some with our paddles, but failed to do so—though the water was only five feet deep. The water on the bar at the mouth of the river we found to be four and a half feet deep, the river half a mile from its mouth being from seventy-five to one hundred yards wide. Soon after reaching the island, a fine breeze sprang up from the north-east, which makes it very pleasant sitting under the cocoa nut trees and indulging in the pleasing reflection that we will not be under the necessity of paddling a second time over this waste of water, as our vessel can not fail to be wafted towards us. We found on the island an almond tree sixteen inches in diameter but little fruit on it. The sail boat having passed us, we concluded to paddle to a village a few miles off, and proceeded but a short distance when the boys expressed a desire to return to the schooner, as she was heading for the north-east, and we were going from her. We gratified them, and it proved fortunate for us, reaching the vessel at 2.30, over a pretty rough sea for our little craft. A native reached the schooner at the same time, who was on his way to Seven Hill Creek, on which Mr. Bennett lives. From this man it was ascertained we were too far south by eight miles.

While returning to the vessel we saw a Chicken hawk, king fisher and snipe, which reminded us of—not home—but the land we left. As we paddled along the coast, before returning to the vessel, numbers of a variety of the sardine, of a beautiful purple and gold color, leaped into the boat. After the scales were scraped from them, they were so near transparent that print could be read though their bodies, though they were more than one-fourth of an inch in thickness. They cooked on the schooner, to-day, a cabbage from the cabbage tree, boiling it with bacon as seasoning, and which was found to be very much like the stalk of cabbage of our gardens, though more tender, yet like all substitutes was very far from the original. This cabbage is nothing more than the pith of the top of the trunk of the Royal palm, and may be obtained four inches in diameter and twelve or fifteen inches in length from a tree that is twenty feet high Reaching the mouth of " Seven Mile " creek, Mr. Morris, Dr. G. A. Frierson and myself proceeded up the creek to the residence of Mr. Bennett, to whom we delivered our letters, and he promised to have at the mouth of the Moho river, 20 miles below Seven Mile creek, for our use, at day-light in the morning, two Dories, properly manned and with competent guides. Soon after we left the vessel a squall came on, with rain, but soon passed off. We were in it long enough to get wet, but are becoming accustomed to that occurrence in this latitude. Here we made our first inquiry concerning the cultivation, or rather growth of corn, yield, &c. Mr. B. stated that he had raised two crops of corn, and two crops of rice in one year. (See article on Cereals.) This place was opened in 1866, the first cutting being done on the 19th of March of that year, and two hundred and fifty acres are now in cultivation, or rather planted in cane ; cultivation is no word in this country. We returned to the vessel after dark, and after reporting progress, it was agreed that the party should be divided ; one to take a boat and explore the Middle River and Golden Stream, and the other the Moho and Rio Grande. The party to explore the first two rivers, near which we were then anchored, to start in the morning with one of the boats, the other to go on with the schooner to the Rio Grande, where they would be left for the expedition up that river, and the schooner to proceed to the "Moho," still farther south, and anchor till all parties should meet again at that place. The party to go above and explore the Golden Stream and Moho rivers to consist of Rev. Mr. Pearce, Mr. Morris, Dr. G. A. Frierson and myself. Mr. Kane went ashore to inform Mr. Bennett of the change in our programme, and we gradually turned to our boards and blankets for the night. Thermometer 6 A. M., 79; 12 M., 82; 6 P. M., 81.

JANUARY 14th.—Though we had a heavy rain last night, there is fair prospect of a good day for our expedition, and by 7 A. M. we were on our way for Middle River, which we found to have 3 1-2 feet water at the bar, with mud bottom, into which the pole would sink very readily to a depth of two feet, which is favorable to navigation, all knowing the difference between grounding on mud and on sand. The river is one hundred yards wide at a distance of one hundred and fifty yards from its mouth, and for a distance of two miles is skirted with Mangrove to the water's edge, which growth is somewhat on the Banyan order, its limbs turning to the water and penetrating the mud at the bottom. The Mangrove for the distance mentioned is small, being not more than eight or ten feet high, but after passing the distance named it increases in size to eight inches in diameter and thirty feet in height. The Mangrove is a certain evidence of of swampy land, though not always found on low ground. For several miles up this river the land is reserved by Messrs.

Toledo & Co., which information we received from one of our party who knew Mr. Bennett, and had been so informed by that gentleman. We found at the distance of three miles from the bar, timber growing to the waters edge, and but little Mangrove. We reached Swazey's landing, which is situated five miles from the bar and on the north bank of the river—at 8. 30 A. M. The bank at this place is three feet high, but at a distance of one hundred and forty yards back rises to an elevation of twelve or fourteen feet. This seems to have been selected by Mr. S. as a site for his houses, on account of its elevation, he being engaged in cutting Mahogany, but being about through, we were informed he would leave for another locality in a few weeks. Here was seen the first hive of stingless bees. They are about one third smaller than our bees, and producing a very fair quantity of honey, for workmen of their size, would be desirable in any locality where they would live. The hive is a hollow log plugged at each end with wood, and of convenient length for hanging against the side of the house by means of vines. When it is desired to take honey, it is done by removing one of the plugs and breaking the cells containing the honey, by repeated punching with a sharpened stick, when the opposite end is elevated and the honey runs out. The hive we saw was four feet long, and had a hollow about six inches in diameter, and is said to yield in February, at which time it is opened, from two to three quarts of honey, by the means stated. After remaining here a few minutes we moved forward. Three-fourths of a mile above Swazey's the north bank rises to four feet, the surface being covered with coarse grass, while the opposite bank is only two feet high. One fourth a mile further on the bank is not more than fifteen or eighteen inches high, the growth being Cahoon and Pimente. Here the river narrows to twenty yards, with an occasional slough coming to it. We passed a tree fallen into the water, on a limb of which we saw drift four feet above the surface of the water, which clearly indicates the stream is not always as low as at present. The place selected by Dr. F. G. Pew, of Arkansas, was reached at 8.30, the Doctor being found busy with his buildings and clearing. The bank at this point is six feet high, and though the stream is eight yards wide we are at the head of even Dorey navigation; the bottom of the stream is rocky with several large rocks cropping out on either bank. From here, north, the guide informed us, the distance is twelve miles to the Golden-stream. Concluding to go a short distance into the country, we crossed the stream at 10. 15 and examined the land for a mile and a half, and returned to our boat thoroughly saturated with water, a very heavy rain having fallen during our trip, from which we had no means of protection.

The ground was very sloppy, and we had some wading to do, though we crossed but one bayou, which will prove an advantage to the ground as a natural drain. Our boatmen, three in number, were as wet as ourselves, but more provident, as they never undertake such expeditions without a "Patikee" in which to carry a change of clothing, and any articles of convenience they may need. The Patikee is a basket made of the splits of a vine called centretie, and in the form of a trunk; the basket sloping upward, in order that the top may fit tightly. These two are covered with palm leaves, and another basket is woven over each, when it is ready for use; not a drop of rain being able to penetrate it.

Bidding adieu to the Doctor at 3 P. M., we moved down the river with the intention of camping near its mouth till morning, when we expect to ascend the Golden-stream. On our way down, seeing a piece of ground about 2 1-2 miles above the mouth that was evidently higher than the surrounding country, and not knowing its extent, we waded across the intervening Mangrove swamp, made an examination and found it to be small in extent, with a large lagoon bounding it on two sides. At 5. 05 our boat landed at a small village, half a mile below the river's mouth, where we remained for the night. After cooking and disposing of our simple meal, and enjoying a cup of tea, furnished by the providence of Mr. Morris, we built a fire and engaged in the drying process, which occupied the night to a late hour. The fire was made of dry Mahogany, and we can testify to its being most excellent fuel, and the only thing that prevented our having a broil was the want of steak, beautiful coals being on hand in large quantity. The native closed his house at dark in order to keep out musquitoes, all that were in the house having been driven out by the smoke. Mr. P. and Dr. F. slung their hammocks, Mr. M. and myself preferring the floor. We slept on a mahogany door, placed without hesitation on the vulgar dirt for our accommodation. Themometer 6. A. M. 79 : 12 M. 78 : 6 P. M. 79.

January 15th.—Left camp this morning for the Goldenstream, finding four feet water on the bar, with mud bottom. For a distance of four miles the shore is very low and covered with Mangrove, after which timber comes to the waters edge and Pimento is very thick. There is also more or less Mangrove which here grows to forty and fifty feet in height and a foot in diameter—would have taken it for something else, but for the opinion of the guide. At the distance of six miles from the bar, came to a boom placed across the river to catch Mahogany logs, which was crossed without difficulty. Seven miles from the mouth of the river there is three feet bank, with cahoon in abundance, the stream being forty yards wide, with twelve feet water.

Half a mile further on we came to another boom, with several hundred Manogany logs, some of them being three feet in diameter and fifty feet in length; which was crossed after very considerable effort and we again moved forward. Antonio (our guide) informed us that he worked at this point for three years, and that as we ascend the river the land will be found higher. Half a mile further up we were at another boom, larger than the one just crossed and so jammed that no opening could be made without great exertion, and would occupy the entire day. Not feeling disposed to be stopped by such obstacles, it was suggest ed to Antonio that we make the attempt to cross, which he did not oppose, we having found him at all times very accommodating, but being informed of another boom a short distance above this concluded to go ashore and examine the country, though we were very anxious to go higher. Landing at 12. 15 P. M., we followed the course of the river through water and swamp for the distance of a mile and a half, frequently wading to our knees, when we came to the boom we were told of, which rendered it ulmost unnecessary to cross the one where the boat was secured. The river is here forty yards wide, with plenty of water, and distance from the bay nine miles. The bank is three feet high at this point, and gradually rises till at a distance of thirty yards from the water's edge, it is about ten feet high. From this place we moved in the direction of Swazey's landing (southward) for a distance of one and a half miles, and found a very good country, covered with Cahoon and an undergrowth, not dense, about the size of hoop poles. Coming to a creek which we found to be deep, and not being able to ford it, returned to the boat and at 2. 45 again turned our faces toward the "briny deep," reaching the camp of last night at 5. 15. Requesting Antonio to make all things ready for our departure at once for the mouth of the Moho, where we expected to find the schooner, he at once proceeded to do so, and at 6 with sails hoisted, though very little breeze, we were on our way and reached the schooner soon after mid-night. On our way down, and when about half an hour out, Antonio boarded the schooner Zenobia, bound for Seven Hills, and the property of Young, Toledo & Co.; he obtained a bottle of Anisette, which caused the blood of the entire party to flow less sluggishly, and brought from "Herardo" and "Simon," two of the crew, several Spanish songs, which, together with our sail down the coast with a very gentle and steady breeze, and the rippling of the water as we passed through it, made the trip one of the most pleasant we will probably make during our stay in the country. Most of the party left on the schooner when we departed for Middle river, had gone up the Moho, and we concluded to camp on shore, and follow them after breakfast in the morning. Thermometer, 6 A. M., 80 1-2 : 12 M. 82 : 6 P. M. 80.

JANUARY 16th.—At 8. 25 we left for the Moho, finding —— feet water on the bar, and the width of the stream two hundred yards from the mouth, to be one hundred and fifty yards, which is preserved for three fourths of a mile. The south bank, for the distance of a mile is skirted with Mangrove which is larger than that found on either the Middle river or Golden-Stream ; the same growth being on the north bank, though smaller.

Three fourths of a mile from the bar a small stream one and a half miles in length, which the natives call "Amargo," enters the river. At the distance of one mile from the bar, timber comes to the waters edge on either side. We tried the temperature of the water and found it to be 76 deg., while the atmosphere was 79 deg. The water is clear and very palatable. One and a half miles from the bar, timber occasionally recedes from the bank for a distance of several hundred yards, the intervening space being covered with Mangrove, which continues for a mile, when timber takes almost entire possession. Not till we had passed over a distance of three and a half miles, did we find Cahoon, and then only one occasionally. At 12 M. we reached the camp of Capt. J. E. Smith, Civil Engineer, who has a number of assistants and is engaged in surveying land for Messrs. Young, Toledo & Co., of Belize. This camp is six feet above the level of the river, but the ground recedes. A short distance below here we landed to examine a native's plantation, containing six or eight acres, where we found growing the Pine-apple, sugar-cane, cassava, yam and Indian-corn; the owner being in the employ of Mr. Swazey and living on Middle river, many miles distant. The river at Camp Dwight, Capt. Smith's present locality, is sixty yards wide and no bottom with a 20 foot line. Rock was occasionally seen jutting from the bank as we paddled along, though none was visible on the surface of the ground. A heavy rain kept us here till 1. 25, when we again pushed out with the hope of overtaking Col. Harrison, who preceded us, having left the vessel yesterday morning, and Camp Dwight at 6 A. M to-day. Previous to to-day we have been surprised at the scarcity of animal life, so much so that the reader will remember our having mentioned seeing several birds, known to us in the States, but a short distance from Camp Dwight we saw the Iguana in immense numbers, and many birds of beautiful plumage which were unknown to us.

Dr. Frierson shot an Iguana that measured nearly four feet in length, the body being about three inches in diameter at its largest part. For the distance of four miles above Camp Dwight the river is fringed to the water's edge with bamboo, and has an average width of fifty yards. Meeting Col. Harrison, we returned with him, reaching the schooner at 6. 20., where the Colonel. gave us the following accunt of his trip. "Found five feet water at the bar, crossed first rapids sixteen miles up, and the second twenty miles from bar, finding two and a half feet water on them and a fall of three feet in one hundred yards; the rapids extending for several hundred yards, no attempt was made to cross them. Here the party landed, and after going two and a half miles north, came to a bayou twelve feet wide, with six feet bank, but land flat and wet. Cahoon was found one mile from bank of river. Several gentlemen went south to the base of a mountain or large hill which was found to be less than a mile from the river." Col. H., when we met him on his return, was in company with several boats containing persons engaged in the same undertaking as ourselves, and whom we did not know, none of whom expressed themselves satisfied with what they had seen. Most of these persons had their camp at Ponto-Gordo, a few miles north of the Moho and on the coast. The expedition up the Rio-Grande was made by Capt. Buckner, Mr. Peak and Mr. Owen. From the Captain we received the following report. "Left the schooner soon after you did, entering the river at 9 A. M., and finding it one hundred and fifty yards wide, one hundred and fifty yards from the mouth, which width it retains for half a mile, where it diminishes to one hundred yards; mangrove growing on either side. One and a half miles up, timber reaches the water's edge on the north side, where the bank was found to be five feet high, which continued about the same heighth as far as "Big-Hills," which are ten miles from the bar. There are two other above this, the first being half a mile distant and the other one mile; at the base of which is an old Spanish settlement, with Cocoa nut and Banana trees growing. (Why was this place abandoned?) These hills are about as high as the seven hills—say one hundred and fifty to two hundred feet. At a distance of sixteen miles from the bar, came to a camp established by mahogany cutters, where the party landed and entered the bush for half a mile, but not finding the land to be what they desired returned to their boat, where a native informed them they could go as far as the rapids, thirty miles above, but no further. From this place they returned to the schooner. Thermometer 6 A. M. 71 : 12 M. 77 : 6 P. M. 77½."

JANUARY 17th.—At 9 A M. our anchor was again brought to the surface and we filled away for Livingston, Guatemala, at the mouth of the Dulce river, which flows from lake Isabel. We saw on this coast the highest land we had seen since leaving Belize ; the mountains frequently coming to the sea. Rain continued during most of last night, but we remained on deck, and succeeded in protecting ourselves pretty well by means of an India rubber coat and umbrella, and in a setting position, slept soundly, as we had often done before. At noon we tried a stewed Iguana, prepared in the most approved style by the schooner's cook, and after laying aside all prejudice, it was pronounced equal to young squirrel in delicacy of flavor. To-day was showery and disagreeable in the extreme. A squall struck us at 1. 20 P. M., which made the little vessel enter the harbor of Livingston with great speed, and we came to anchor at 1. 40. At the time of our leaving Belize there was some cholera reported at the place, which was not unknown at Livingston. Soon as we anchored a health officer came aboard, and we were informed it was necessary for us to go into quarantine, for several days, before we could come on shore. This was a disappointment, as we desired to visit lake Isabal, and to ramble over a little high ground, but could not think of subjecting ourselves to the modest requirement of several days quarantine. Not being able to go ashore we succeeded in replenishing our stock of fluids with several bottles of native rum, though the person who brought it out could not tread the deck of the vessel. Presume the health officer thought he was perfectly safe along side—we sincerely hope he is still living. As this section of the world is said to be infested with snakes, and alcoholic liquor being considered in our land a specfic for their bite, on the principle of alcohol not being digested, but passing off through the circulation, and one poison neutralizing another, we can confidently recommend the rum of Livingston for the purpose named, as we certainly never tested such villainous stuff before, during the whole course of our lives, not excepting the *Pine top* of Confederate times which it leaves in the shade as completely as the "God of day" does the refulgent beams of a farthing rush light. Thanks, however, to the gentleman who was kind enough to obtain it for us, it was undoubtedly the best he could do. We also obtained of Mr.—— a bunch of fine fish which were the first since leaving Belize: having failed in all our efforts to catch any by trolling as we sailed along the coast. Livingston seemed to be a very small place, we saw only a few houses, near the bluff, on which it is situated, and which is from twenty to thirty feet in height. At 4 o'clock, the stiff breeze from the north-west that prevailed at the time we cast anchor having subsided, we moved away from Livingston in the direction of Omoa, in the Republic of Honduras. Thermometer, 6 A. M. 72; 12 M. 75; 6 P. M. 74.

JANUARY 18th.—A heavy rain this morning at an unseasonable hour stirred up the deck sleepers, and the water was so rough that several of the party were sea-sick. As we sailed along, the coast presents the same appearance as at and near Livingston, the mountains coming to the sea. We ought to have reached Omoa during the night, but did not till a late hour in the afternoon, and while rapidly approaching the harbor the captain was hailed from a small boat, in a language we did not understand, but its magic effect was at once visible, for never did anchor of the same weight reach bottom quicker in the same depth of water than did that of the "Three Sisters," and we were still. Horror of horrors, the authorities are afraid of cholera,—but will see us in the morning. Visions of quarantine rise before us, shutting out from our view all that is beautiful, and crowding from the memory all that is hopeful. One thing we felt assured of, if they wanted a cholera germ at Omoa, it would only be necessary to keep us in the Pig-sty we were occupying and they would get it of the most virulent type. We determined to go ashore the next day, if not at Omoa, at some other place. For some days past nearly every hygienic law has been transgressed, and for the first time in our life we were inclined to doubt that "Disease is in many cases consequent upon the violation of a law of nature." Thermometer 6, A. M. 77; 12 M; 78½; 6 P. M. 79.

January 19.—We passed a very disagreeable night, having frequent showers, but were cheered by the sun's appearance at 7.30, and we proceeded to "hang out" our clothes, blankets, &c. Having left nearly all our baggage at Belize we frequently find it difficult to raise a dry garment when the rain continues. The celebrated fort of Omoa is within a short distance of us, but the town is half a mile back, and looks rather *small for its age.*

At 8 A. M., Dr. De Soto, the health officer came on board, and finding each individual in possession of a cup of coffee and hard tack concluded we were all right, and returned to report. In an hour and a quarter, seemingly a very long time, permission was granted us to go ashore, of which we were not slow to avail ourselves, and very soon all were once more on *Terra firma.* We "put up" at Belisle's Hotel, and had the best of the season placed before us in the greatest variety and prepared in the most approved styles. Belisle or as he is called by most persons the "Judge," is quite a noted individual—holding several offices of a civil character, and is the only hotel keeper in the place. You are not roused from your slumbers by the discordant gong, or the unpleasant bell, but by the dulcet notes of a very large hand organ, which is played with great skill by the judge himself.

We have yet to hear of the first person going to the Judge hungry and leaving unfed, or going without money and going away empty. We were the recipients of many kindnesses from the Judge, in the case of articles left with him, and in other ways, and on all occasions found him equal to any trust confided to him. We reached shore in time for breakfast, which, according to the custom of the country is placed on the board at 10 A. M., coffee having been served at 7, and which is considered sufficient foundation, but confess we always felt, before the breakfast hour, that our foundation would hardly support the superstructure we expected to place upon it.

At 1 P. M., Col. Harison and myself obtained horses and under guidance of a gentleman who had visited the coast, made a trip to "Port Cabellos," about ten miles distant, and the northern terminus of the projected interoceanic railroad that is to run from the bay of Farseca on the south, and which was surveyed by Mr. Trautwine in 1858 at an expense of two hundred thousand dollars. The length of route surveyed being about one hundred and fifty miles. We passed on our route a tree of gigantic size said to be the one under which Cortes gave "*Gracias a Dios*" for his escape from the many perils by which he was beset in his travels. The port is situated at the head of a beautiful bay and has one of the finest harbors in the world; maps prepared in England from coast surveys, shew that the largest vessels can anchor within a very short distance of the coast in perfect safety, and small craft can come within one hundred yards of the shore. Col. McDermott and several others we found at this place, who intend locating near by, but had not, we believe, positively decided where. The colonel seemed very enthusiastic, and we certainly hope he may realize every expectation. At 4.30 we started on our return for Omoa, but in consequence of the character of the road over which we had to pass, much of it being at the beach, and the surf rolling in very heavily, concluded to stop for the night with the magistrate of *Cienagueta*, Mr. Robinson, who placed before us for supper, coffee, wheat bread and *fried Panot*. We are learning to eat what is placed before us, and seldom ask questions. The Panot we found to appear and taste much like the flesh of the Dorey; the meat on its breast being quite an inch thick, and very tender. We have tried to eat Panot since then, and to place ourselves right and not to appear to occupy a false position, will state that they were invariably so tough that parboiling and hashing were necessary to enable one to think of attempting to digest it.

On the route between Omoa and the port it is necessary to pass through two Carib villages. Cienagueta and Tulian, and to cross the Tulian and Marquez rivers, the first by fording and the second by boat, leaving your horses behind. This river runs from the Marquez Lagoon, immediately in rear of the port, and flows into the sea less than half a mile below. There are also several mountain streams of small size, all of which together with the Tulian, have rapid currents over rocky bottoms and the water very clear, cool and palatable. Thermometer 6 A. M., 76; 12 M., 80; 6 P. M., 77.

January 20th.—At 7 this morning we again made a start for Omoa, stopping on the way to examine a Coffee Estate, or Rancho, which was the first we had seen. (For description see "Productions of Honduras") We were informed on this trip that the Chamlicon river could be navigated to within three miles of San Pedro Sula. If it is so, why pass over the mountains? We will make further inquiry on this point. The road for two miles from Omoa was very sloppy, and when we reached town, at 9.10, we looked as though we had just made an extensive trip over a hitherto unexplored Louisiana swamp in the rainy season, and had several times lost our way. Having quite a quantity of clothing that rubbing as well as wetting will improve, several of us repaired to the Omoa river to see what improvement we could make in their appearance. We washed and spread on the rocks, and by the time the last was spread the first were ready for the ironing room. In the afternoon, Dr. Gray, Dr. Ryan, Rev. Mr. Pearce and Mr. Morris engaged a Dorey and started, the first for lake Isabal, Dr. Ryan for Porto-Gordo, where he left his family, and the Rev. Mr. Pearce and Mr. Morris for Belize, via "Seven Hills."

The rest of us, except Dr. G. P. Frierson and Mr. Daniel Swett, who will remain here, or endeavor to reach San Pedro via the Chamlicon river, hope to get off to-morrow, taking the mule and mountains as our mode of conveyance and route. Col. H., Dr. F., Mr. D. S. and myself paid our respects to-day to the Commandante of Omoa, Genl. Espanoza, by whom we were very kindly received, and who expressed great satisfaction at the prospect of our citizens emigrating to the Republic; making known to us that land could be obtained gratis, and if we should be so fortunate as to find an unclaimed *gold mine*, that the authorities of the nearest municipality would cause to be surveyed a certain distance north, east and west, of the point we should designate, which would establish our claim. It is hardly necessary to say we did not have any surveying done. Thermometer 6 A. M., 72 ; 12 M., 80½ ; 6 P. M., 78.

JANUARY 21st.—At 9 o'clock this morning we were mounted and off for the far famed San Pedro Sula, and reached the Rancho Grande, eighteen miles distant, at 3 P. M., where we had the pleasure of meeting Mr. Reynaud, owner of the premises, and Governor of the Circuit of San Pedro ; and saw the operation of winnowing coffee to remove the husk, which is done by the ordinary fan mill, which we found on examination to have been made by Allen & Co., of New York. Here we saw coffee in every stage, and were informed by the Governor that he has forty-five hundred bearing trees, producing, he can not say how much, but will know at the close of the season, as he is keeping an accurate account of the crop as gathered. (See productions of Honduras.) The residence at the Rancho is constructed in a very substantial manner, of brick, plastered inside and out, and covered with tiles. The plantation is in a bowl, surrounded by mountains, and is said to be twenty-five hundred feet above the level of the sea. The Rio Grande, about forty yards wide, clear and cool from the mountains, flows by a short distance from the house, and is easily forded, To-day has been cloudy with occasional showers, and though the thermometer indicates 77 deg. at 4 o'clock P. M., our feelings are decidedly in favor of fire, which would be very comfortable. Thermometer 6 A. M. 74, 12 M. 74½, 6 P. M. 73½.

JANUARY 22d.—Left Rancho Grande at 7 this morning, reaching the foot of the mountains on the opposite slope at 9.10, and moved along their base for a distance of fifteen miles through a beautiful avenue formed by the branches of the Cahoon Palm that gracefully curve over the road, in many places entirely shutting out the sun's rays. Stopped at the village of Chiloma, on the Chiloma river, for breakfast at 10.40. We found here the Umbrella China tree growing in perfection, which we never saw in Mississippi, though it is planted in Texas for its shade. At 12.30 P. M. we were again in the saddle, and crossed the Rio Blanco four miles from San Pedro, which we found to be forty yards wide, very shallow, sandy bottom and water warm and very unpalatable ; the Thermometer indicating in the atmosphere 83½ and in the water 89 deg., time 2.30 P. M. Two miles frem San Pedro we crossed the Mermijo, fifteen yards wide, and about twelve to eighteen inches deep—the same as the last two crossed—water clear and bottom sandy. Several fields of Corn were passed by us, and a field of Cotton, entirely stripped of foliage. Our journey terminated at 3.20, and we found ourselves in a place where the houses did not prevent our seeing the town. Through the kindness of Mr. Reynaud we were provided with an excellent dinner, to which we did ample justice. Thermom. 6 A. M. 70; 12 M., 79 ; 6 P. M., 78.

JANUARY 23d.—We breakfasted at 11 A. M., though coffee was served at 7, mounted our mules at 12, and accompained by Maj. G. Malcolm rode around to inspect the country ; following the Comayagua road, running south from San Pedro, for half a mile, at which point we left it, moving to the east-crossing the Tipiaca two miles from town and following the same road to the Rio Blanco, four miles from town, beyond which the land is claimed by Mr. Debrot, of Omoa. On our way back we passed a cotton field which we were informed was without leaves three weeks ago, but is now in full foliage, though the genuine *Army worm* is again at work and will soon have it stripped once more. The country over which we passed is very flat, with Cahoon the prevailing growth, though the soil contained a very large proportion of sand. The rivers above named are quite small, being from fifteen to twenty yards wide at the time we visited them, and about two feet deep, with sandy bottoms, though the water was not very clear nor cool, but palatable. We reached San Pedro in time for dinner at 5; the order of our meals will in future be as follows: Coffee at 7, breakfast at 11, dinner at 5. Thermometer 6 A. M., 75; 12 M., 78½; 6 P. M., 78.

JANUARY 24.—At 8.30 this morning we were again on the way to continue our explorations, Maj. M. again accompanying us. Our object to-day being to strike the Tacomiche river immediately below the junction of the Tipiaca and Blanco, which form it. The general direction of these rivers is south-east, and their waters flow to the Chemlicon, the general direction of which is north-east to the Gulf of Honduras. After passing over the road pursued yesterday for two and a half miles, we turned to the south-east, crossing more wet land than we expected to see, and passing over quite a large piece of ground covered with very coarse grass growing from three to four feet high. Our conjectures were that a swamp must be near, and though we had a guide and several men armed with the Machete to cut the way, our fears were soon realized; our horses moving forward with difficulty, which increased till necessity compelled a return. On the way out, the animals we were riding fell, but rose without our dismounting, and despite their exertions, fell again, and being unable to rise we dismounted and waded out, when the course was changed further to the south, which we followed till satisfied we were on a large body of good land when we struck for the Comayagua wood, which was reached two miles from San Pedro. From this point several of the party returned to town, while Col. H., Capt. B., Dr. F. and myself concluded to visit the Chamlicon river, said to be five miles distant. On our way we crosed the La Puerta, three miles from town, which is a very small stream, and a few hundred yards beyond turned to the left in order to follow the Comayagua road, the other crossing the mountains close by. The river where we struck it is from seventy five to one hundred yards wide, with two and a half feet water on the rapids at this point, and has all the characteristics of mountain streams, being clear, cool and drinkable. After enjoying the *luxury* of a bath, we retraced our steps toward San Pedro, meeting our *Chef de cuisine,* whom the Colonel had sent back to obtain refreshments for the inner man. Seating ourselves on the grass a hearty meal was soon made on eggs, corn bread and beef. It may be well to state that this proved to be the first and last time we had corn bread placed before us during our stay in Spanish Honduras, and up to this time have seen no preparation of flour since leaving Omoa.

After our meal, Col. H. and myself started for the mountains, two and a half miles east of San Pedro, but the day being far spent, with every prospect of rain, returned to our quarters. The distance from San Pedro to the Chamlicon by the Camayagua road is seven miles; three miles of the way being almost entirely level, and could with little labor be made an excellent carriage road. Beyond the " Puerta " the road is very rocky for most of the way to the river. The land seen to-day is generally better than that seen yesterday, covered with cahoon and having several naturul drains running through it. At the Puerta musquitoes annoyed us very much, though we were not troubled by them yesterday nor to-day up to this time. We have found bars unnecessary to our comfort at San Pedro, not having seen, felt or heard a musquito at that place. Thermometer 6 A. M. 73½; 12 M. 82; 6 P. M. 78.

JANUARY 25.—Our attempt to reach the Tacomiche yesterday proving unsuccessful, though it is reported to be only five miles from San Pedro, we were again in the saddle this morning at 8, to try another route, which we did by keeping a general course to the southeast from San Pedro till we reached what the natives call the Tipiaca mountain, about five miles from San Pedro, and no river being in sight we deemed it best to return and adopt some more certain method of accomplishing our object. On our way this morning we passed an old plantation of 62 Cocoa trees quite full of fruit. Over a considerable portion of our route to-day the country presented the appearance of once having been in cultivation, and on making enquiry concerning it, we received the assurance that such was the fact. Why was the cultivation of this section discontinued by those who burnt the bush and ate the produce of the soil perhaps a century ago? The land examined to-day was found to be of every character known to this country, except rocky; at times covered with cahoon, and high and dry, with very rich soil; and at other times lower and wet, with the same growth, when it changes to a gravel sub-soil but a few inches below the surface, and at times to portions covered with heavy grass. We have frequently been surprised to find so large an admixture of sand where it was reasonable to expect but little, though the growth even on such land was very heavy, and the cahoon nearly always present in greater or less quantity. On our return to San Pedro we were much disposed to think the guide, who has made two unsuccessful attempts to convey us to our point of destination, unreliable, and it was determined to employ another, who said he could find the river, if we would furnish him with men to assist in cutting, and pay him if he accomplished his object; if not, no pay. Many lime trees were found to-day, the fruit being quite as large as the lemons imported into the United States. The natives being thirsty drank from a *water vine*, a piece of which, four feet in length and three inches in diameter yielded a pint of very palatable fluid, devoid or any green or sappy taste, which quenched the thirst very quickly. This morning was showery, and we were alternately wet and dry, though we feel no inconvenience from it. Thermometer 6 A. M., 72½; 12 M., 81; 6 P. M., 73½.

JANUARY 26.—This morning we saw the first fog since leaving Belize. At 12 M. Col. H. and myself, accompanied by Dr. Scott, who has for seven years resided at San Pedro, visited the site of old San Pedro, two miles south-west of the present town of that name, which we found overgrown to such an extent that we saw nothing more than the remains of what we were told was the wall surrounding the place at the time of its destruction. We moved on to where the *Rio de los Piedras* issues from the mountains, and following its course for a mile we crossed a stream known as *Santa Anna*, and at a distance of two miles from here, following the base of the mountains, we came to the *Mermijo*, at the point where it comes from the mountains. All these streams are clear, cool and very rapid, although small. The *San Pedro* and *Rio de los Piedras* unite about four miles from where the latter makes its exit from the mountains, and not far below this the Rio de los Piedras unites with the Mermijo, near where the latter crosses the road from San Pedro to Omoa. Nearly all the country between San Pedro and the mountains, on the west, *has at some time been under cultivation*, but is now covered with undergrowth, except where small clearings have been recently made. Thermometer 6 A. M., 72; 12 M., 81½; 6 P. M., 76.

JANUARY 27.—This morning, at 8.40, Messrs. Kane, Owen,

Peak and Dr. G. A. Frierson left us on their return to Omoa, the first two intending to extend their trip to the United States, but soon to return, and the others to proceed to Belize for baggage left there by the entire party.

William, our *chef de cuisine*, accompanied Mr. Owen to Louisiana, but expressed his determination to return, and thought he would be able to bring others with him. Dr. F. and Mr. D. S. not having made their appearance, we have written to them to make the attempt via the Zequisiesta, which empties into the Chemblicon, and is stated to be navigable for Dories to within fourteen and a half miles of San Pedro, whither we will send mules for them as soon as we hear of their having left Omoa ; the road being represented to be good. We will take a rest to-day, and hope to-morrow to be able to visit the *Zacomiche*. Thermometer 9 A. M., 69 ; 12 M., 78½ ; 6 P. M., 77.

January 28.—At 8.20 this morning our entire party was again in the saddle, Maj. Malcolm accompanying us, and we were off for the Zacomiche, which was *discovered* yesterday, crossing the *Tipiaca* two miles east of town, and taking a course east by south, we reached the river at 12. 10, about seven miles from San Pedro, and found it to be eight yards wide and three and a half feet deep. This is the river we were told would be navigated by a *steamer* to be brought out on the next trip of the Tradewind. Most of the land passed over was found to be much the same as that already described. At the water's edge we found musquitoes, but none as we approached the river, and as singular as it may appear, we took a nap within twenty yards of the water and were unmolested by them. Several Iguanas were seen to-day, the first we have found since leaving the Moho in British Honduras. Most of the party engaged in fishing catching several cats and one of a kind known to the natives as "Sleeping-fish," which was very much like the cat in appearance, but having scales.

Captain Buckner took the guide with him and endeavored to reach the mouth of the river, which was supposed to be close by, but after going three miles, without success, gave it up and we all returned to San Pedro as soon as he rejoined us. Thermometer 6 A. M. 67 : 12 M. 85 ; 6 P. M. 81 ; 9 P. M. 75.

JANUARY 29th.—This morning we accompanied Maj. Malcolm to his kitchen garden, where kale, mustard, turnips, tomatoes, snap-beans, okra, pumpkins and black-eyed peas, were found growing and looking well. His cotton field was also visited, and plenty of eggs found to produce another supply of worms, and but a few days can elapse before they will be at work, and the destruction of foliage is but a question of time, and a very short time at that ; notwithstanding, Maj. Malcolm and many whose fields have been stripped, still think they will make half a crop. Thermometer 6 A. M. 71 ; 9 A. M. 81 ; 12 M. 86 ; 3 P. M. 88 ; 6 P. M. 80 ; 9 P. M. 78.

JANUARY 30.—To-day being showery and very disagreeable, we kept within doors. In the evening, though the Thermometer indicated 70 deg., we made a fire and sat near it with great comfort. Thermometer 6 A. M. 71 deg. 9 A. M. 72 deg. 12 M. 72 deg. 6 P. M. 70 deg. 9 P. M. 67½ deg.

JANUARY 31st.—The bad weather continuing, we made a feeble effort at visiting on a small scale, but most of the time kept our room, as rain fell at intervals during the entire day. Thermometer 6 A. M. 64 ; 9 A. M. 65 1-2 ; 12 M. 69 1-2 ; 3 P. M. 70 ; 6 P. M. 72 1-2 ; 9 P. M. 70.

FEBRUARY 1st.—No rain this morning, though the atmosphere is damp and chilly to such an extent that our fire is kept up, and with the party around, it reminds us of camp. We saw to-day Irish potatoes, grown here from seed brought from the States, which were of respectable size, but are said to be inclined to be watery, though the sweet potato does well, according to report. By invitation we visited the field of Mr. —— Jack, where the sarsaparilla was seen growing, though none had up to this time been gathered. Though there was some prospect at an early hour this morning of a fair day, we have had repeated showers. Thermometer 6 A. M. 65 ; 9 A. M. 68 ; 12 M. 70 1-2 ; 3 P. M. 71 1-2 ; 6 P. M. 71 1-2 ; 9 P. M. 70.

FEBRUARY 2d—A courier was sent to the gentlemen who remained behind when we left Omoa, several days since ; he should be back to-day, and his failure to appear will necessitate a trip to that place, to carry out the object for which he was sent. To our great astonishment, Mr. D. S., and Dr. F., and two sons made their appearance this afternoon, having crossed the mountains, on mules. As one of the riders weighs two hundred and forty pounds, he can best tell how the trip was made, though the mule would undoubtedly have something to say if endowed with the power of speech, for his weight did not greatly exceed the burden he had to carry. These gentlemen left Omoa on last Wednesday, 29th ult., but were detained at the Ranche by bad weather till this morning. Thermometer 6 A. M. 68 1-2; 9 A. M. 69 ; 12 M. 72 ; 3 P. M. 74 ; 6 P. M. 72 ; 9 P. M. 71.

FEBRUARY 3d.—A Dorey said to be drawing two feet, arrived this morning at the village of Chemlicon, on the river of the same name, within seven miles of San Pedro, loaded with freight from Cienagueta. We were told nine days were required to make the trip ; our efforts to obtain the particulars of the trip were, however, entirely unsuccessful. Colonel H., Dr. F., and Mr. D. S., accompanied by Dr. Scott, who kindly offered his services as guide, made a trip to the mountains west of San Pedro, returning late in the evening drenched by rain which fell heavily during the day.

This may not be the "rainy season," but it is certainly a season of rain. Thermometer 6 A. M. 68 1-2 ; 9 A. M. 72 ; 12 M. 75 ; 3 P, M. 72 ; 6 P. M. 77 1-2.

FEBRUARY 4th.—Our party explored the country to-day between San Pedro and the mountains west, finding some excellent land between the Los Piedras and Mermijo, though on the latter, and for some distance from its right bank it was found to be very sandy. This exploration was made on foot, with compass in hand, and though we had two natives to use the machete found the trip very fatiguing and will not soon be caught making a similar one. We returned to San Pedro at a late hour, but the bath and change of clothing could not be deferred, for we are well acquainted with the Agarrapata. This is a very good place to describe this pest. It is nothing more than the wood tick, called by some "seed-tick." They are so small as almost to require a magnifying glass to make them visible, and figures would fail to make their number known. Any one going to the woods is certain to return with thousands of them. We always adopted every precaution against them, such as tying the pants close around the ancle and brushing off repeatedly with a bunch of twigs. We have seen the most fearful effects produced by them where these precautions were neglected. It is said they are not troublesome for more than two months in the year, but we were unable to ascertain what two months. Perhaps the sixty days you are supposed to be *absent* from the place were referred to. Thermometer 6 A. M. 68 ; 12 M. 75 ; 6 P. M. 78.

FEBRUARY 5th.—Colonel H., Captain B. and myself endeavored to ascend the mountains to-day in order to get a view of that portion of the valley of Sula, in which San Pedro is situated; our horses were used as far as possible, when we dismounted and began the ascent, walking till tired, resting and again pushing on, which was repeated, though we did not succeed in reaching the top. An elevation was attained, however, that gave us a magnificent view of the valley below, seemingly stretching to the east for twenty miles and to the south to nearly double that distance. But for the rain and clouds we would have had a better view, but we were amply repaid for our toil. Mr. D. S. had a chill to-day, which is pretty good evidence this latitude can produce the "Bilious Intermittent." Thermometer 6 A. M. 74; 12 M. 78; 6 P. M. 76.

FEBRUARY 6th.—We are still unable to exclaim, "Behold how brightly breaks the morn," for rain is again falling, and the heavens are entirely overcast. The rain continued during the day with a short intermission at noon. Thermometer 6 A. M. 74; 12 M. 82; 6 P. M. 78.

FEBRUARY 7th.—A miserable day was this to the writer, as the "Bilious Intermittant" culminated and he shivered. Perhaps he did not wish he was home! His bed was a blanket spread on not a large quantity of shavings, which had a dirt floor foundation. Why did'nt he go to the Hotel? Hotel! Let us drop this subject. Mr. D. S. is now quite well, but when sick it required the united efforts of two individuals for forty-eight hours to secure a hide bottomed bedstead, for which it was agreed seventy-five cents per month should be paid. Thermometer 6 A. M. 69.

FEBRUARY 8th.—Rain again to-day. Having heard of several persons being down with chills, we are naturally led to inquire into the cause. Is it the rain, change of weather, heat, fatigue, or is it the result of malarious influences? Being unable to say, we can only testify to the complaint being, if not the most dangerous, the most disagreeable disease known to the human family, and persons here not unfrequently have them of the quotidian type for a week at a time. All emigrants are requested by Gov. Reynand to meet at the *Cavildo* (Court-house) to-morrow morning, to hear read a translation of the concessions made by the Puebla (town) of San Pedro Sula, for their benefit. Information has reached here of the arrival of sixty-four persons at Omoa, destined for this place, and quite a large number being at Belize, also coming here.

FEBRUARY, 9th.—Notwithstanding we should look for a chill to-day, visited the Cavildo, remaining but a short time, as we have not only heard the concessions read, but have a copy in the original, in our possession.

FEBRUARY 10th.—Thermometer 6 A. M. 67 1-2 deg. 12 M. 82 1-2 deg. 6 P. M. 80 deg.

FEBRUARY 11th.—Thermometer 6 A. M. 67 1-2 deg. 12 M. 83 deg. 6 P. M. 77 1-2 deg.

FEBRUARY 12th.—Having kept quiet during the past two days, and no repetition of our chill, feel pretty safe for the present. All complained of having slept cold last night notwithstanding blankets and closed doors. Information was received this morning of Mr. Peak and Dr. Frierson, who have arrived at Omoa with the baggage and supplies of the party, will come forward via the Chemlicon and Tequisiesta as soon as they can make arrangements for so doing. It is their intention to bring the freight to a point within fourteen miles of San Pedro, from which it will be brought here by wagon, there being two of those very convenient vehicles for the conveyance of goods at this place, and plenty of oxen. Thermometer 6 A. M. 64 1-2 ; 12 M. 79 ; 6 P, M. 70.

FEBRUARY 13th.—To-day information was received that Mr. P. and Dr. F., left Omoa several days since and ascended the Chemlicon to the Taquisiesta, when, in consequence of low water and obstructions in the river, they returned to the bar at the mouth of the Chemlicon, there to remain until instructions should be received from here. All were much disappointed at this delay, as they have been without their Sunday clothes for nearly six weeks. Thermometer 6 A. M. 74 ; 12 M, 80 1-2 ; 6 P. M. 76.

FEBRUARY 14th.—It was decided this morning that Captain Buckner and myself should take a Dorey and men at the ford of the Chemlicon, seven miles south-east of here and proceed to the bar of the river and assist the gentlemen in charge of the baggage, they having had a serious time of it since leaving Omoa. Our preparations were hastily made, and cousisted of blanket, bar, mackintosh, india-rubber coat and jerked beef; our dependence for bread being the plantain, a quantity of which we intended taking with us from the crossing, and to replenish our stock as needed at the various plantations we expected to pass. The Captain and myself left San Pedro at 10 A. M., and at 11.30 reached the village of Chemlicon, and presented the letter kindly furnished by Gov. Reynaud, and which expressed the desire that we should be furnished with two men and a Dorey for the trip. Our main dependence was a man named John, who it was ascertained after considerable delay, was in San Pedro, consequently we must await his return. On our way back to re-cross the river we visited a hot sulphur spring, not more than thirty yards from the river's bank, the temperature of which we could not ascertain, having left our thermometer at San Pedro, but it was evidently very high, steam being distinctly visible even at noon-day as the water bubbled up. We will endeavor to visit this spot again, and get a bottle of water for analysis. When we recrossed the river, John was on hand, but of course could not think of making a start till morning, this being the natives' peculiar habit in all such cases, and having sent our horses back, will remain here till morning, at which time there is fair prospect of our getting an early start. Thermometer 6 A. M. 73 ; 12 M. 76 ; 6 P. M. 78.

FEBRUARY 15—At 6.30 we were off, and although we expected to have John only, or two men at most, find a boy in the boat whose duty will be to use a pole. At 7.40 a point was passed known to the natives as Juarlomo, though nothing was in sight save a girl washing clothes ; and at 8.15 an island, and at 8.30 another neither of which contained more than three or four acres ; and at 8.45 another, about 10 acres in extent, the growth on which is principally willow. The mouth of the *Tacomiche* was pased at 11, and the Cow pen reached at 11.30, (This point is known as the Cow pen, because it was used in years past as a place for assembling cattle for the use of Mahogany cutters.) Nearly opposite this place one of the boatmen owns a plantation and the boat was stopped there in order that a supply of plantains might be laid in for the voyage. The Cow pen is situated at the base of quite a large hill, and the bank is from eight to ten feet high. We pushed out at 12 M., and at 2 passed a piece of ground on our right that had the appearance of an immense clearing, covered with high grass, and hardly a tree on it, and appeared to contain several hundred acres. The same character of country was seen a few miles below, but the patches did not seem so extensive. John informed us that though this ground is covered with grass, and peat, it is not swampy. Want of time prevented our making such an examination as we desired, but at 2.45 we went ashore to examine, by climbing a tree, this peculiar and not uninteresting country, and to ascertain to what extent a kind of willow existed that was occasionally seen. Over thousands of acres the grass extends with here and there an isolated willow, the bank at the waters edge being four feet high. Was this district of country cleared by man ; and if so, why is it not now made to produce something for his support ? For several miles we passed through country that presented much the same appearance, the grass being on either shore—the bank three feet high and river fifty yards wide. At 3 P. M. we left the main river and entered a "cut off" at our right. (This cut off was made by a raft in the river a mile or two below, which entirely prevents navigation by the main stream,) we passed over a foot fall in entering the "cut off" which at this place is ten yards wide eight feet deep, and has a current of about *seven miles* an hour. The utmost skill was necessary on the part of the boatmen to avoid running into the bank and against fallen trees, or sunken logs, and to prevent our being dragged into the water by overhanging limbs. At 3 P. M., a piece of low marshy ground was reached, and an occasional Mangrove seen—depth of water four feet. As good camping ground is not easily found, availed ourselves of the first that offered and at 5 stopped for the night. Thermometer, 6 A. M. 71 : 12 M. 72 : 6 P. M. 73.

FEBRUARY 16th.—Left camp this morning at 6.30. The stream here is about twenty yards wide, but as we advanced, would at times become narrow, and in the course of the morning we passed over portions not more than four yards wide, and over several miles that did not exceed six in width, and a current varying from five to seven miles an hour. During the time we have been in this stream, no paddling has been necessary except for the purpose of avoiding obstructions. At 9 we made our exit from this "cut off" and again entered the main river, where but little current was found. Width of river fifty yards and bank twelve to fifteen feet high for a short distance, when it falls to six and eight feet. For several miles we passed through country similar to that seen in the cut off, and covered with high grass and willow, and being miles in extent from the river as well as along its banks. At I.30 we stopped at a plantation, cut some sugar cane—picked up some lemons and again moved on. (When the word *plantation* is used, do not think it refers to thousands of acres, as they vary in size from *one to ten acres.*) Distant mountains have been visible on our left during the entire day, but at this place they come to the water's edge. While passing through the cut off we saw thonsands of Iguanas, and many birds of all kinds known to this section, except ducks of which but few were seen ; and alligators constantly plunging into the water or swimming along the bank.

At 5 o'clock, our boatmen beginning to talk about camp, a promise of tobacco if we reached the bar that evening induced them to keep the paddles in motion, and our trip ended precisely at 6 o'clock. Having made the trip in 26 1-2 hours running time. We left San Pedro in the rain—slept in the rain last night—sat in the rain to day from time of leaving camp to 2 P. M., and we are cold and disagreeable in the extreme. The fires that were visible as we approached the bar had a very comfortable appearance, and the chilly wind blowing from the sea caused us to seek their warmth at a double quick. We found a norther prevailing at the time of reaching the bar, and a very heavy sea running and breaking on the beach with tremendous force, which renders it impossible for boats to cross the bar and to go to Cienagueta. In crossing the bar one of the boats containing baggage was swamped, wetting all it contained, and ruining many articles. A courier left San Pedro on the morning of the 14th for this place, but has not yet arrived, though he expected to come through in one day. He is doubtless at Cienagueta, awaiting a change in the weather, which will probably not occur for several days. Thermometer, 6 A. M. 68 : 12 A. M. 72 1-2 : 6 P. M. 79.

FEBRUARY 17th.—Rain again this morning—wind continuing, and sea as rough as yesterday. All seem to be in doubt as to the best course to pursue, and find it difficult to decide whether it would be best to try the river as far as the " Cow Pen," (beyond which there are five shoals with only one foot water on them) or to return to Cienaqueta and try the mountains. By 9 A. M. the wind changed to the north-west, with an occasional shower, and the sun showing himself at noon, all hands engaged in drying wet clothing and other effects, which had been nearly completed on the previous day by Messrs. P. and F. It having been decided to try the river, preparation was at once commenced for the trip; two dories were engaged for the purpose, one of which when loaded will draw twenty inches and the other sixteen. This movement will be carried out unless information is received from San Pedro to stop it. Nothing heard of the courier. Thermometer 6 A. M., 68; 12 M., 71; 6 P. M., 70.

FEBRUARY 18th.—Rain again this morning, with heavy clouds at the north and west which present an angry appearance. Our blankets were wet again last night by the rain beating through our Cahoon shelters. After considerable exertion and great waste of patience we succeeded in making a fire, which we find as necessary for warmth as for culinary purposes, and perhaps more so, as the stock of provisions is not in great variety and the services of a Soyer is not needed in the kitchen. At 9.30 wind changed to the south, with rain falling heavily, and but little prospect of abatement. The natives cooked a Baboon to-day, but we know nothing of its flavor. We have eaten Conch, Iguana, and other things that did not present a very inviting *appearance*, but *no Baboon*. At 1 P. M. wind changed to the west—the rain ceased, and we again made a fire and dried, or attempted to dry what had again received a wetting. At night the clouds disappeared, as usual. The sea continues very rough, and the roaring of the surf as it lashes the beach might be heard for several miles. Thermometer 6 A. M., 67 ; 12 M., 69 ; 6 P. M., 69.

FEBRUARY 19th.—To our great joy the sun rose clear this morning, and we feel anxious to make a start, but must wait for men from Cienagueta. It is always delay with these people, who have no idea of the value of time, except as a means of measuring distance from one point to another. The sea being smoother this morning, a boat started for Omoa for provision for the men in charge of the effects of passengers who came by the last trip of the Steamer. Their effects are in bad order, having been wet for several days. Our individual baggage was returned from this place to Omoa, by the boat, as we expect to leave San Pedro immediately on our arrival there, for the United States. The courier that left San Pedro on the morning of the 14th reached here at 10.30 A. M., having been detained at Cienagueta by bad weather, as we expected. The men expected from Cienagueta arrived in time to load the boats and be off by 1.45, P. M. They are to receive for transporting three thousand pounds of freight from here to the " Cow Pen," a distance of sixty-seven miles, forty-three dollars, payment to be made in currency, which is not greenbacks. The river was ascended for about eight miles, and camp pitched for the night. Thermometer 6 A. M., 65 ; 12 M., 73 ; 6 P.M., 71.

FEBRUARY 20th.—At 6 this morning we were again on the

way, which is an early start for these people, though we should have been off an hour or more earlier. The bank at this place is three feet high, with plenty of Cahoon, and soil exceedingly rich. At 7 the heavens were overcast with "Mackerel Sky" which is a very good sign of rain, and the growling of a Baboon which was heard before we left camp, was pronounced by one of the boatmen a certain indication of "falling weather." At 7.55 a point was passed where a raft will soon be formed, as the passage is only ten yards, while the stream is seventy-five yards in width; fallen trees having nearly closed it. The large boat got across the first log that has retarded our progress, at 8.40, when a line was taken ashore and in a few minutes she was off. By 9 the sky was perfectly clear, which was cheering, as we have no tarpaulins with which to cover our effects, and if they again get wet it will be a more serious undertaking to dry them than was the case at the bar. At 11 the plantation was reached where we obtained lemons on our down trip, and we again stopped to lay in a supply of plantains, lemons and sugar-cane. Our large boat stuck on a log at 3 P. M., but was not detained more than five minutes—the men taking water and dragging her off. In consequence of our being near the grassy region, and the terminus of Cahoon growth on this side of the "cut off," stopped at 4 and pitched camp, where it will be necessary to cook rations for two days, as we will soon be in a country where it will be almost impossible to find a camp. To-morrow we will be in the cut off, when the *work of the trip* will begin. Thermometer 6 A. M., 60; 12 M., 76; 6 P. M., 74.

FEBURARY 21st.—We are afloat this morning at 5.30, which is an improvement on yesterday's start. A heavy fog hangs over the river and it is quite cool. The cut off was entered at 9 A. M., the boat occupied by Captain B. and myself going ahead, as we have the pilot. The boats are all provided with poles and paddles, the first being constantly used after we left the river. Our boat camped at 5.40, near a place where the current was very swift, which point was not reached by the other boats; the large one camping three-fourths of a mile below us, and the cedar boat lower down. Thermometer 6 A. M., 63; 12 M., 80; 6 P. M., 78.

FEBURARY 22d.—The large boat reached our camp at 6.40 this morning, and stopped to prepare provision for the day. The cedar boat is not in sight, yet we are not anxious concerning it, as the men in charge have shown great energy, and one of them is the best boatman of the party. At 7.20, all hands having breakfasted we were again on the way. At 10.40 we reached our camp of the first night going down. Considerable detention was caused at 12 M. by the large boat getting across another log, which occurred again at 12.45. This log had to be cut in order to effect a passage. We are making very slow progress against current, logs, stumps, vines and the overhanging branches of trees. At 3.20, our pilot finding we were in a lagoon, and consequently out of our course, it became necessary to turn back a mile in order to re-gain the right direction. We had hoped to be out of this flat country and once more among Cahoon, before night, but now think there is little chance of our doing so. At 5 P. M. the large boat grounded, and was relieved by all hands taking to the water and manning the gunwales, Camp was pitched this evening at 5.30, in a very disagreeable place, the cedar boat being a short distance ahead and the large boat about one hundred yards below us. Thermometer 6 A. M., 63; 12 M., 79½; 6 P. M. 76.

FEBRUARY 23d.—6 o'clock found us on the way this morning, and we think from our locality we are about two miles from the main stream. At 6.15 the big boat was stopped by a log which it was found nec essary to cut under water, and was again halted by a similar cause at 6.45, in a very rapid current. At 7.20 we reached a point where the river is almost entirely closed by a large tree lying across it, the only passage being a circular one worn by the current around the roots, which the large boat was *exactly large* enough to pass. At 8.05 all three boats were at the mouth of the cut-off, and in half an hour entered the Chamlicon, over a very rough place, tied up to rest for a few minutes, and again moved on. While our boat was being quietly poled along, at 10.50, the boy leaped into the water, and after a momentary scuffle, rose to the surface with a turtle weighing about eight pounds. We could see no indication of anything of the kind, and the water was not clear enough for the bottom to be seen. This beats any fishing we have seen, and proves a decided independence of hook and line. Our boat reached the Cow-pen at 4 P. M., the large boat at 5, but the cedar boat did not come up to-night. Thermom., 6 A. M., 63 ; 12 M. 79 ; 6 P. M. 76.

FEBRUARY 24th.—Captain Buckner and myself left Camp this morning for San Pedro, at 6.30. A note was discovered here last evening written by Col. H., who was here on Saturday (22d), which states the distance to San Pedro to be twelve miles. For several miles after leaving the Cow-pen our route lay over a rolling country; after which we came to a piece of prairie land with here and there a clump of small live oaks. This piece seemed to contain about two hundred acres, and is covered with coarse grass from two to three feet high. This being a high, dry, and rolling piece of ground, we asked ourself the question, was this ever in cultivation? This trip will long be remembered by Captain B. and myself, as we left camp with baggage enough for a pack-mule of small dimensions, and though we slung it to a pole, and tried the shoulders, and this hand and that, keeping step with military precision, we failed to lessen its specific gravity. *En route,* the Blanco and Tacomiche were waded, the first two feet, and the second one foot deep, and we reached San Pedro at a late hour in the afternoon, where terminated one of the most fatiguing trips in which it was ever our misfortune to engage. Distance from S. Pedro to Cow-pen, thirteen miles, and from Cow-pen to bar, sixty-seven; total distance eighty miles. We will have occasion to refer to the river again. Thermometer, 6 A. M., 66; 12 M. 82; 6 P. M. 78.

FEBRUARY 25th.—A party is on the road between San Pedro and the Cow-pen, cutting the way wide enough for wagons, which is necessary to be done in a few places. Col. H. is with them to point out where certain advantageous changes may be made, as he examined the road a few days since. Thermometer, 6 A. M. 70; 12 M. 82; 6 P. M. 72.

FEBRUARY 26th.—As we expected, the man engaged yesterday to go to the Cow-pen for our baggage did not get off till this morning. *Extra* payment induced an earlier start than they are in the habit of making, and exacted the promise to be back this evening. He may arrive before morning and enable us to get off as we desire—but, patience! "We will see what we will see." A native was found last evening secreted in the house of an immigrant, and was tried, sentenced and punished by 12 M. to-day—receiving one hundred strokes with stout tamarind switches; in addition to which he will be required to work for the public a given length of time. *Mardi Gras* has been in operation here for the past two weeks, and on Monday last the *Trudor* sports should have begun, which are carried to a considerable extent in Brazil by throwing flour on each other, and by throwing against the person their waxen bottles filled with scented water. We saw no flour used in that or in any other manner, but a few persons used a small compressible metal bottle, throwing the water by squeezing the bottle. The individual who went for our baggage, returned this evening, which is wonderful indeed; but the person engaged to carry it to Omoa says he cannot start till day after to-morrow. We will endeavor to remove every obstacle to his going. Thermometer 6 A. M. 69; 12 M. 82; 6 P. M. 70.

FEBRUARY 27th.—Our baggage is ready, but not until the sun was an hour high did the party engaged to carry it make his appearance. He came to get money with which to purchase rations, Mr. D. S. having promised to feed him on the road, and also raised the price he at first charged, from two dollars to two dollars and fifty cents. Twenty-five cents being given him to procure rations, the work of tying on *two trunks* was commenced, three persons being engaged in it, which was completed to their satisfaction in half an hour. Ropes always have to be furnished for this purpose by the owner of baggage. Mr. Lucius Middlebrook and Mr. D. S. made a start at 8.10, and the baggage man at 8.30; we leaving San Pedro at 9.45, and overtaking the other gentlemen before they reached the mountain, the ascent of which was begun at 2.25 and terminated at Rancho Grande, at its foot, without accident, at 5.15 P. M.

The following being posted at Rancho Grande, is copied for the benefit of "all whom it may concern."

For ranging beast per night .... 6¼ cts.
For use of bed with net (no bedding is furnished, C. S.)..50
" " without net..........................25
One meal at regular meal hours..... ....37½
After 7 at night, each meal, each person............50
One cup of coffee, with biscuit 12½

Those who do not wish to occupy beds, may have the free use of the Hall.

(Signed) REGINO PREO, Proprietor.

FEBRUARY 28.—At 6 this morning, we again mounted our mules and moved in the direction of the coast, congratulating ourselves on the fact of this being the last day over this miserable road. The day proved cloudy and without rain, which made the trip much more pleasant than would have been the case under a clear sky. We reached Omoa at 2.10, and the Judge's dinner hour being 4 P. M. we repaired to the Omoa river to exterminate the last *agarrapata*.

FEBRUARY 29th.—We engaged passage, and embarked on schooner Omoa, bound for Belize, at 1.15. During the afternoon and that night hardly a breath of air stirred, and we could not tell whether we were moving, Mr. D. S. has another chill, and we can only hope he will be as fortunate as on a former occasion, and have but one.

MARCH 1st.—No breeze to-day except of the most gentle character, and we are yet a long distance from our destination. The sun again disappeared beneath the horizon without our seeing Belize, though the trip is often made in twelve honrs.

MARCH 2d.—Belize is in sight this morning, and we came to anchor at 12.30. A customhouse officer came aboard immediately, and permitted us to go ashore at once. We "put up" at Brewer's Hotel, Captain T. C. Brewer, proprietor. It affords us pleasure to be able to say the captain is an ex Confed. and a gentleman, and that you will always find the *Table d'Hôte* supplied with the best the market affords, and at reasonable rates. The sleeping apartments are neat, airy and comfortable. Patronize him if you visit Belize, aud you will not go away dissatisfied.

MARCH 3d.—Jas. M. Putnam Esq., agent for Messrs, Young, Toledo & Co., extended an invitation to us to accompany him to the Moho river, or rather the "Cattle Landing," two miles north of the mouth of that river, for which place he expects to start this evening with the steamer Enterprise, belonging to the firm mentioned, and will carry down a number of persons who arrived on the last steamer from New Orleans. We made our preparation for going, but the vessel did not make her appearance during the day.

MARCH 4th.—It is ascertained that the Enterprise is aground at the "Haul Over," which is a water connection between the Belize river and the Bay. The steamer had been in the river for some time undergoing repairs, and could only enter the Bay by the route named, on account of a bridge spanning the river in town. Quite a number of gentlemen who were waiting here for her, are gone this morning to tender their services in getting her off. Thermom. 6 A. M. 79; 12 M. 83; 6 P. M. 79.

MARCH 5th.—The "Enterprise" succeeded in getting off the bar this morning and reached her anchorage in the harbor at 7.20 A. M. The "Trade-wind" will sail on the 7th, and we have abandoned the trip to the Moho, as it is two late for us to make it and return in time for the steamer, the distance being ninety miles. We paid our respects this morning to his Excellency, Gov. Longdon, and spent an hour both pleasantly and profitably with that gentleman. Having been informed of a grant made to an American Company, of an extensive piece of country lying between Monkey and Deep rivers, we made inquiry of his Excellency concerning it and found it was not as we had heard. The "Enterprise" sailed this evening at 6, with a large company. Thermometer 6 A. M., 77; 12 M., 81; 6 P. M. 76.

MARCH 6th.—Several gentlemen on their way to the States

arrived at Belize this morning from San Pedro. They informed us that a party had visited the Ulua river at its nearest point to San Pedro, eighteen miles, and that they reported six feet water to the bar of that stream. How they arrived at that conclusion we are unable to say, as we were not told they descended the river. We remember distinctly that, before we descended the Chemlicon it was reported to have two and a half feet at its lowest stage. Thermometer 6 A. M., 77 ; 12 M., 80 ; 6 P. M. 79.

MARCH 7th.—The wind has been blowing briskly from the east for several days, and we anticipated rough weather on the trip, but having made every preparation for the voyage, hope to pass the time more comfortably than from New Orleans here. The "Trade-wind" weighed anchor at 12 M., and we are off for the land of *Leafless trees*. At 1.25, in consequence of roughness of the sea on the "outside" cast anchor and remained here till morning. Thermometer 6 A. M., 77 ; 12 M., 81 ; 6 P. M., 78.

MARCH 8th.—Anchor was weighed this morning at 6, and we are again on our way. In a few hours we were useless to ourselves, and of no service to any one, and might have been found occupying the upper berth in No. 9, which we kept not only to-day, but the next, and *the next*.

MARCH 11th.—We are able to be up to-day, but feel as though we had passed through a severe attack of sickness. We think a roe herring would be good—none to be obtained—cranberry jelly—none within reach. "Waiter, have you any mackerel?" "I believe it is *all gone*, sir, but will see." "Mackerel, sir!" "Ah, thank you." Better mackerel we never ate, and a good breakfast was made though the quantity eaten was very small. Tried a cigar, but succeeded in making a very small quantity of ashes. Took a chew, nauseating weed! how can any one use it? We retire to our room, lie down, and endeavor to decide which would be worse as a punishment for a person who is liable to sea-sickness—a compulsory sea faring life, the penitentiary, or decapitation....

MARCH 12th.—Crossed the bar at 9.30 A. M., and reached New Orleans at 10 P. M., remaining on board till morning.

MARCH 13th.—By 12.30 baggage was delivered, and we are busy getting ready for the Jackson cars, which are to leave at 4 P. M. instead of 7, as was the case a short time since. We succeeded in making a start, and will reach " Old Warren," at 10.30, on the morning of March 14th, 1868.

BRITISH HONDURAS.

It is singular, but true, that few persons who have not visited Belize, have any well defined or correct ideas of that place. Of all the passengers on the Tradewind when we went over, there being more than a hundred, only two or three persons, who had visited the country, had any other idea of the place than that the houses were rudely constructed, and the principal portion of the population about as rude as the buildings. We confess our surprise was great, when first we caught sight of the town, at night, but greater was our surprise, when we viewed it in the morning, and found that it extended along the shore for a distance of more than a mile, with well built houses and palm trees scattered here and there, waving their umbrella like tops to the breeze, and relieving the monotonous white of the buildings by their foliage, presenting a very beautiful and fairy-like scene. The town has a width of less than half a mile, with a Mangrove swamp extending along its rear, and is drained by the Belize River, which places the northern end in an island made by the water of the river passing through the "haul over" six miles from town. There is a canal running the entire length ot the place, and in rear of it, which is twenty-five feet wide, piled on either side, and spanned by several *iron* bridges. The streets are of good width, without sidewalks, and are kept scrupulously clean. No matter how hard it may rain or how windy it may be, there is no mud in the one case, nor dust in the other, as the streets are made of sand and small gravel, and are so hard and smooth as to present the appearance of cement or concrete walks. The Customhouse is an excellent building, and has a beautiful wharf, close by; the market house, though not large, is constructed of iron, and the bridge which spans the river is a very substantial structure, though built of wood. The houses are from one to three stories high, and are constructed of brick, frame, and a few of corrugated iron; and are covered principally with slate, tile and iron. Most persons do business on the lower floor and reside above, where may be found apartments as neatly constructed and as elegantly furnished as at any other place we can name. The merchants of Belize are able to drive their business, and not let their business drive them, for at 4 o'clock P. M. every store of any pretensions is closed, with a promptness that caused us to ask if it was in accordance with law, and were informed it was simply a custom. (Happy merchants, thought we, if you do not do business on twelve months' time. If you lived in the United States you would think slavery still in existence, as with us there is certainly no class of men who are worked harder than the merchants.) There are six churches; two Episcopal, one Methodist, one Baptist, one Catholic and one Presbyterian. All very neat and large for a place the size of Belize; the Methodist being very handsome indeed. We will endeavor to give a short description of it. The corner stone was laid by Gov. Austin, November 3d, 1864. The building is constructed of brick, with slate roof, and covers a surface of about 50x100 feet, and has two floors, the lower one with ceiling about fifteen feet high, which is used as a school-room, and the upper for Divine service; a stair-case running from the outside of the building, being the mode of reaching it. The pews are of Mahogany, and the pulpit is of the same material; large, and circular in form, with a handsome lamp on either side of the cushion and two in rear. In rear of the pulpit are three tablets, six feet high and three in width, those at the sides containing the Ten Commandments, and that in the centre the Apostles Creed. Gothic windows of green glass occupy nearly the entire width of the building, at the end where the pulpit is situated, and on either side of the room double gothic windows of colored glass, with circular windows above them, extend from floor to ceiling, which is a gothic vault, with a base one half the width of the building, and from which two arches gracefully curve to the walls. The ceiling is painted white, and is relieved by strips of mahogany, several inches wide, running from base to apex, at intervals of about three feet. Five chandeliers with three lights each, are suspended from the roof, and eight lamps at the walls, four on either side. We found by calculation that the floor would hold four hundred and fifty-six persons, and the gallery one hundred and eight. We attended service here at night, two hundred or more of the colored population being present, and only *three white persons*, that we could see, and we never saw a more quiet or attentive congregation. The moment we appeared at the door, we were politely conducted to a seat, and every attention shown that could anywhere be given.

There is considerable business done at Belize, though we are inclined to think from the appearance of stocks in store that too heavy a preparation has been made for the immigrants' accommodation. There are few roads around the town, and not many in the country generally, transportation being carried on with boats and pack-mules. A boat is almost as indispensible to an inhabitant of this place as a carriage or buggy is with us, and they seem to have exhausted their skill and ingenuity in their construction—some of them being very artistically and elegantly made. There are several kinds of boats, the most important being the "Dorey" and "Pitpan." The first is shaped like a ship's boat, and sharp at both ends, and the second is very long for its width and is used for navigating shallow water. These boats are made of a single piece of wood, and are what we would call "canoes, or dug-outs."

LAWS.

Concerning the laws it is hardly necessary to say anything, as they are *English*. Suffice it to say, that, here law prevails, and this is one of the most orderly communities we have ever visited.

LANDS.

Those who have followed us this far will be able to form a pretty correct idea of the soil, and its location, and only a few words are necessary on this point. The idea prevails that there is very little thin land, which is not the case, as we not unfrequently found clay at a depth of eight inches, and much land containing too large a proportion of sand. The cahoon palm which is received as a sure indication of rich land was found growing on soil both wet and dry, rich and poor. That there is high land in British Honduras cannot be questioned, but it is not on the coast, nor is it on the rivers within fifteen or twenty miles of the coast, anywhere south of Belize that was visited by us, except at 'All Pines' and 'Seven Hills,' and we were informed the best lands could be found in that part of the colony. We examined the lands on the rivers; and as far as examined, they are generally flat, and present every indication of being subject to overflow. We found high ground on the Middle River and Golden-stream, and have no doubt there is a ridge of land between all these rivers that is above overflow, but what is extent, and what is the character of the country between those points and the rivers, or the coast?

RIVERS.

The rivers of the colony examined by us are truly beautiful streams, almost entirely without obstructions, and generally very deep. The Golden-stream, Rio-Grande, and Moho might be navigated for twenty miles at least, by the Mississippi River steamer General Quitman, when once over the bar, and at high tide she would have no difficulty in passing that point.

REPTILES AND INSECTS.

During our stay in British Honduras, we saw but two snakes one of which was killed by Dr. F. on the Golden-stream, and the other we saw at All Pines; the first being unknown to us, and the second a garter snake. Mosquitoes, sand flies and bottle flies, except when the sea breeze prevails are very numerous and innoying. The first is an old enemy, and the second not unknown in this country, but the third belongs to a different atitude—we will describe it. In size it is almost the same as the urkey gnat, and punctures the flesh, usually without causing pain, eaving as its mark a small red spot of blood drawn to the outer ayer of the skin. For eighteen or twenty-four hours this does ot annoy, but at about that time an itching sensation is proiuced, and you scratch continually, when the hands swell considerably, presenting a very unnatural appearance. We were rtunately told to puncture those spots as soon as discovered, ress out the blood and bathe with salt water, which was done, id no unpleasant results followed their bite. We have seen indreds of these bites on the hands of a single individual. nts are very numerous and destructive to gardens. Housees, so familiar to us, are here almost unknown.

FRUITS.

The orange, lemon, lime, plantain, banana, guava, pine-apple, cocoa-nut, and we might add all the fruits of the tropics, *in their season*.

VEGETABLES.

Much the same as with us, and in addition the yam, yampa, casáva, coco or malanga, and others of less importance. The yam is very much like our sweet potato in appearance, and grows to a large size, frequently weighing ten or fifteen pounds; and when boiled, very closely resembles the Irish potato. The yampa is also a root, but does not attain the size of the yam, and is in taste a medium between the Irish and sweet potato. The casava and malanga are also roots, the first of which grows to the weight of four or five pounds and has already been described, and the second to the size of our Irish potato, and is the nearest approach to that vegetable of all we have named.

CEREALS.

Corn is grown, and according to report, two crops are raised in one year. We were shown some of this grain at Seven Hills, the ears being of medium size and full to the ends. It is very farinaceous and is early attacked by weevil, that in a short time leave nothing but husk. Many persons claimed that not only two crops a year can be raised, but sixty bushels an acre to the crop. We saw nothing that promised a larger return than fifteen bushels but we did not measure either land or corn.

Of rice we saw some that was very fine. Two crops a year are also claimed for this. We are satisfied this is a very fine country for its production, and that the yield will be both large in quantity and excellent in quality.

THEABROMA CACAO.

This tree, from the fruit of which the chocolate of commerce is made, we did not see growing in British Honduras, but *heard of one* south of Belize, and of a patch of twenty or more on the Belize River. Parties who have tried it say they did not succeed well with it.

COFFEE.

Did not see a tree growing in the colony. A gentleman of my acquaintance said he did not believe there was a tree in British Honduras, but was told there was *one at Corosal.* We know of no reason why both coffee and cacao will not grow here equally as well as in Spanish Honduras, and believe if proper locations are selected and the necessary care and attention are bestowed they will succeed.

DOMESTIC ANIMALS.

Of horses, mules, cattle, hogs and sheep, there are very few in the country: Spanish Honduras and Guatemala being depended on as the sources of supply.

GOVERNMENT OFFICERS.

His Excellency, Lt. Gov. Jas. Robt. Longdon. Private Secretary, Fredk. Harcourt Hamblin. Col. Secry., Controller of Customs, and clerk to the Council, Lt. P. J. Hankin, R. N. Col. Secretary, Austin Wm. Cox. Col. Treasurer, Antonio Mathé. Attorney general, Joseph H. Phillips. Bishop, Bishop of Kingston. Chief Justice, Hon. R. J. Corner. Crown Surveyor, J. H. Faber. Immigration Agent, A. W. Cox, and many others; the above being the most important.

The Legislature is composed of the Lt. Governor and a Legislative Assembly of twenty-one members, viz., eighteen elective and three nominated by the Crown, also an Executive Council of six members.

Executive Council, (styled honorable,) Officer Com. troops, Col. Secretary, Treasurer, Attorney-General *Ex Officio*: A. W. Cox, A. Mathé, P. Toledo.

Imports of the colony for 1866............. £169,033 08
Exports 277,155 16

American Consul.................... A. C. Prindle.
Spanish Honduras.................... J. E. Mutrie.

Census population of colony, April 7, 1861........ 25,635
Present .. .. Belize about.............. 6,000
The population of the colony, including the towns, is almost entirely colored.

DUES.

On the effects of agricultural immigrants there is no duty; but such persons on their way to Spanish Honduras will be required to pay "Trans-shipment dues," varying from twenty-five to fifty cents per package; the latter to be paid for each barrel of flour and pork.

Many being under the impression that "living" is cheaper at Belize than in the United States, the following from the "Belize Honduras Colonist" of February 29th, 1868, will enable them to form a better idea perhaps than they at present have of the subject. Gold or silver to be used in payment.

FINANCIAL AND COMMERCIAL

Rate of Exchange of Bills on England is $500 per £100 sterling.

MARKET PRICES.

Flour	$14 to 15 per bbl.
Rice	$5 to 6 " 100 lbs.
Corn	$1 to 1.12½ per bbl.
Plantains	26½ to 75c. " 100.
Yams	$2.25 to 2.50 " 100.
Beef	$18 to 25 per bbl.
Butter	44 to 50c. " lb.
Lard	14 to 16c. " "
Pork, Prime	$24 per bbl.
" Mess	$24 to 25 per bbl.
Fish	$6 to $7 " 100 lbs.
Fowls	$4.50 to 6 " doz.
Sugar, brown	$7 to 7½ " 100 lbs.
" white	$16 to 19 " "
" loaf	$18 to 21 " "
Coffee	18 to 20 " "
Tea	$1.25 to 1.50 per lb.
Tobacco, leaf	25 to 32 " 100.
Cedar	25 to $40 " M. ft.
Pitch Pine Lumber	35 to $40 " "
White Pine	40 to $45 " "
Mahogany boards	$80 " "

Before taking up the subject of Spanish Honduras, it is a pleasure to add our testimony to the fact that his Excellency, Jas. Robt. Longdon, Governor of British Honduras is a gentleman in every way qualified for the position he fills with so much satisfaction to the people of the colony, and that he possesses the rare combination of an excellent administrative and executive officer, the result of large experience and close observation, which, together with a finished education, polished manner, and earnest desire to promote the welfare of those under him, has greatly endeared him to all.

We found him also to be eminently practical in his ideas, and trust if this should meet his eye, that he will excuse our using an expression made use of by him, and which we will not soon forget, "that he did not so much desire to hear what persons could do, as what they had accomplished" in their planting operations.

SPANISH HONDURAS,

OR

THE REPUBLIC OF HONDURAS.

Perhaps Spanish Honduras, particularly San Pedro and vicinity, received attention from our countrymen at as early a day as British Honduras. Major Green Malcolm, of Kentucky, left Atlanta, Georgia, in April 1867, for San Pedro, via Omoa, with seventy souls. Soon after their arrival at San Pedro it was decided to place the government of their local interests under the control of a council, in order to avoid the necessity of assembling the entire colony when any question of interest or expediency should arise likely to effect their welfare, and at a public meeting they elected as their council the following gentlemen: Maj. Malcolm as their presiding officer.

G. Malcolm,	L. G. Pirkle,
H. H. Briers,	Geo. W. Walters,
J. H. Wade,	P. Goldsmith, Secy.

MEDINA.

The site for a town to be called Medina, in honor of the President of the Republic, was selected soon after the arrival of Major Malcolm, but up to the time of our leaving San Pedro it did not contain a finished house, and only three or four were in course of construction. The site selected adjoins the corporation of San Pedro. In May, 1867, Major Malcolm was made Inspector of Foreign Immigration, the following being a copy of his commission from the Government.

(*Copia*) COMAYAGUA, Mayo 8, 1867.

Senor GREEN MALCOLM.

El Gobierno en atencion a que V. ha sido admitido ya como ciudadano de esta Republica, y teniendo en consideracion sus aptitudes y buenos deseos por la prosperidad del pais, ha tenido a bien nombrarle por acuerdo de hoy Inspector de la Inmigracion estrangera en la costa é interior del departamento de Santa Barbara, debiendo V. dar cuenta al Gobierno de las disposiciones que adopte afin de cumplir con el encargo que se le confiere, para allanar las dificultades que se presenten y disponer todo lo que sea conveniente en el particular.

Esperando que V. se servira aceptar este nombramiento, tengo el placer de suscribirme de V. muy atento servidor.

PONCIANO LEIVA.

Hay un sello del Ministerio de Relaciones Interiores y Gobernacion.

Es conforme al original.

San Pedro, Febrero 2, 1868.

J. REYNAUD.

(TRANSLATION.)

(*Copy.*) COMAYAGUA, May 8, 1867.

Mr. Green Malcolm,

Sir:

The government, considering that you have already been admitted as a citizen of this Republic, and satisfied of your abilities and good wishes for the prosperity of the country, has deemed it expedient to nominate you by a resolution passed this day, Inspector of Foreign Immigration for the coast and the interior of the Department of Santa Barbara, making it your duty to report to the Government, whatever measures you may adopt, in your official capacity, to remove all difficulties that may arise and to promote the views of Government on the subject of immigration.

Hoping that you will accept this nomination, I have the pleasure to subscribe myself yours respectfully,

PONCIANO LEIVA.

Given under the seal of the Ministry of Interior Relations and Government.

A true copy,

San Pedro, February 2, 1868.

J. REYNAUD.

On the third of May, 1867, the communication below was forwarded to the authorities.

(*Copy.*)

To his Excellency the President and Executive officers of the Republic of Honduras;

GENTLEMEN:

The undersigned respectfully submits to your consideration, that on the 10th of April, after a passage of ten days, I arrived in the city of Omoa with seventy souls, emigrants to your beautiful land. These persons consist of men, women and children, who are what might be termed the forerunners of perhaps thousands of the best citizens of the Southern States, of the United States. We wish to make this our home. To find in this that which we have lost in our own native land, liberty. To make this what our country was before it was destroyed by our enemies. Our desire is to become citizens of the Republic at once, to be a part of your people, to claim your protection, to defend you with our lives from foreign invasion, and to do our whole duty to our adopted country. In coming among you we would state that on account of our recent great misfortunes, many of us are greatly impoverished, and without going into further preliminary remarks, would give this as our reason for asking you to grant the following privileges and donations.

1st. A grant of land as indicated in the accompanying map.

2d. A free port at Port Acabellos for three years, for the exclusive benefit of the colony.

3d. The exclusive navigation of the rivers Chamilicon, Ulua and their tributries for ten years.

4th. The right to build roads through public or private lands, for the benefit of the Colony and Government.

5th. The right to construct aqueducts and bring water through our and adjacent lands.

6th. The exemption from taxation for two years from the day of arrival.

7th. The privilege of enacting our own municipal regulations in conformity with the laws of the Republic.

8th. The privilege of organizing our city adjacent to San Pedro, separately from that town and naming it the city of Medina.

9th. The exclusive privilege of establishing manufactories for the manufacture of woolen and cotton goods in the Repnblic for ten years.

10th. The exclusive privilege of introducing for five years, wagons, buggies and carriages, the common sense sewing machine, washing machines of all descriptions with machines for making tin-ware.

11th. The privilege of distilling liquors from the productions of our farms. The privilege of planting and harvesting all seeds in our colony, and introducting the still known as the "Log still."

12th. The privilege of introducing for eight years the circular saw mill run by steam or water, planing machines and shingle machines. The above we acknowledge appears liberal and we would not have you think us asking too much, for we by these privileges and grants, desire and are determined as far as possible to use them to the improvement, development and welfare of the country as well as ourselves.

With the highest consideration,

I am gentlemen, your obedient servant.

(Signed.) G. MALCOLM.

Comayagua, Honduras, C. A., May 3, 1867.

To which the following answer was returned.

(*Copia.*)

El Presidente en quien reside el Supremo Poder Ejecutivo de la Republica de Honduras, por cuanto : Haberse presentado el Senor Green Malcolm natural de los E. E. U. U., por si y a nombre de varias familias sus connacionales, solicitando establecerse en el territorio de la Republica bajo el gose de los ciudadanos Hondurenos y con sujeccion a las leyes vigentes y que en lo succesivo se emitan en el pais, para cuyo intento piden varios privilegios y conseciones.

Considerando—Que la Republica necesita de inmigrantes industriosos para desarrollar los elementos naturales de riquezas que abundan, y que el Decreto Legislativo de 23 de Febrero de año pasado faculta al Gobierno para protejer esta clase de empresas. Por tanto ; ha venido en hacer y decretar las conseciones :

1a. Se permite a los inmigrantes honrados y laboriosos procedentes de los E. E. U. U. del Sur de la America de Norte que han llegado y que arriben en lo succesivo a pais, el establecimiento en el Distrito de San Pedro, Departamento de Santa Barbara, de una poblacion, que llevara el titulo de ciudad de Medina.

2a. A mas del uso comun que la Municipalidad de San Pedro ha concedido a dichos inmigrantes en sus ejidos bajo las condiciones asignadas en una acta que ha presentado en copia e Senor Malcolm, y que el Gobierno ha aprobado, se les concede los terrenos nacionales contiguos a los ejidos de San Pedro asi a Sur de dicha poblacion y contenidos dentro de estos limite principales : El Chamalecon, la Cima del Cerro nombrado l Cumbre y la base de las montanas del Sur Oeste del mism pueblo ; debiendo oportunamente practicarse una delineacion adecuada.

3a. El Puerto Cortés sera franco por tres años para que los pobladores de la ciudad de Medina introduscan todo lo que les sea necessario para su consumo y establecimiento de casas, fabricas, maquinas, etc.

4a. La navegacion por medio de vapor o fuerza de caballos, de los rios de Chamalecon, Ulua y sus tributarios sera esclusiva para los mismos inmigrantes por el termino de ocho años.

5a. Se les concede tambien los siguientes privilegios esclusivos : 1o. Por diez anos el establecimiento de maquinas para manufacturar lana, algodon, u otras materias fibrosas, y para refinar azucar. 2o. Por ocho años el de maquina circular movida por agua o vapor para acerrar madera y la de acepillar y hacer tejamani. 3o. La introduccion por cinco años de carros, calezas, carruages, la maquina de cocer conocida con el nombre de " Common Sense Sewing Machine," la de hacer bajilla de lata, y el alambique conocido con el nombre de " log still " para la destilacion y venta de licores, la haran de conformidad con los reglamentos de este ramo.

6a. Tendran el derecho de construir caminos que pasen por terrenos nacionales o de propriedad particular para beneficios de ellos mismos y del Gobierno y el de hacer acueductos o traer aguas para regar sus terrenos.

7a. Los pobladores de la ciudad de Medina estaran excentos del servicio militar y de contribuciones forsosas por el termino de dos años contados desde su arribo al pais.

8a. Tendran el derecho de elejir para su Gobierno local y con arreglo a las leyes de la Republica un cuerpo municipal, pudiendo entre tanto haya un numero de quinientas almas, ser rejidos por un Gobernador y un Juez de Paz que elegiran de entre ellos mismos, estando subordinados el primero al Gobernador de Santa Barbara y el segundo al Juez de Primera Instancia de Omoa.

9a. Tendra el derecho de hacer sus reglamentos municipales o bandos para el Gobierno Interior de la poblacion de conformidad con las leyes de la Republica y sometiendolos a la aprobacion del Congreso, o del Supremo Poder Ejecutivo.

10a. Los articulos que dichos pobladores embarquen en los puertos de la Republica, seran libres de todo derecho de exportacion por el termino de ocho años. Estas concessiones en nada perjudicaran a la empresa del Ferro-carril Inter-Oceanico, proyectado, pues los privilegios permitidos o que se permitan sobre este particular seran una excepcion de estas concessiones.

Sera entendido, que los privilegios antes referidos relativos al establecimiento de maquinas, se extenderan solamente en los departamentos de Santa Barbara, Gracias y Comayagua, excepto el de la maquina de hacer telas que sera extensivo a toda la Republica.

Si dentro de tres años no hubiese en la ciudad que va a fundarse un numero de quinientas almas por lo menos, los privilegios concedidos en este Decreto quedaran sin efecto ; pero en este caso los inmigrantes que ya esten establecidos disfrutaran de la propriedad de la parte que tengan cultivados de los terrenos concedidos. Escritas en Comayagua en la casa de Gobierno a ocho de Mayo de mil ochosientos sesenta-y-siete.

J. LOPEZ,

PONSEANO LEIVA.

Hay un sello.

Es conforme con su original.

San Pedro, Enero 29, 1868.

J. REYNAUD.

(TRANSLATION.)

The President, in whom resides the supreme executive power of the Republic of Honduras.

Whereas, Mr. Green Malcolm, a native of the United States, for himself and in behalf of various families of his nationality has presented a petition, soliciting permission to settle in the territory of the Republic, with the privileges of citizens of Honduras, and subjecting themselves to the laws now in force or that may hereafter be enacted in this country, with which intent they ask certain privileges and concessions.

CONSIDERING

That the Republic is in need of industrious Immigrants to develop the natural resources which abound in our country, and that the Legislative Decree of 23d February of last year authorizes the Government to protect this class of enterprises;

Therefore, now makes and decrees the following concessions;

1st. It is permitted to the honest and industrious Immigrants from the United States, of the South of North America, who have already come or may hereafter come to this country, to establish, in the District of San Pedro, Department of Santa Barbara, a cummunity which shall bear the title of City of Medina.

2d. Besides the common use which the Municipality of San Pedro has granted to said Immigrants in its public lands, under the conditions laid down in the Act presented by Mr. Malcolm, and which the Government has approved, they are also granted the national lands contiguous to those of San Pedro towards the south, and included within the following boundaries; the Cham-icon and the base of the mountains of the south-west of the said village of San Pedro, a delineation of which will be opportunely made.

3. Port Cortes shall be free during three years, in order that the settlers of the city of Medina may introduce everything necessary for their consumption, and for the establishment of houses, manufactories, machinery, etc.

4. Navigation by steam or horse power of the rivers Chamlicon, Ulua and its tributaries, shall be the exclusive privilege of said Immigrants for a period of eight years.

5th. They are also granted the following exclusive privileges:

1st. For ten years, the establishment of machines for manufacturing cotton, woollen and other fibrous goods, and for refining sugar.

2d. For eight years, the establishment of steam or water power mills, for sawing and planing lumber, also wash machines.

3d. The introduction during five years, of wagons, buggies, carriages, the sewing machine known as the "Common Sense Sewing Machine," the machine for making tin-ware and the still known as the "Log Still," for the distillation of spirituous liquors, and the sale of the same, under the regulations relative to this branch.

6. They shall have the right of constructing roads over national lands, or lands of private persons, for the benefit of themselves and of the Government, and to construct aqueducts to conduct water for the irrigation of their lands.

7. The settlers of the city of Medina, shall be exempt from military service and forced contributions during two years from their arrival.

8. They shall have the right to elect for their government, and in conformity with the laws of the Republic, a municipal body; and may, in the meantime, and until they number 500 persons, be ruled by a Governor and a Judge of the Peace whom they shall elect from among themselves, those officers being

subordinate, the former to the Governor of Santa Barbara, and the latter to the "Judge in the First Instance" of Omoa.

9th. They shall have the right to make their own rules and regulations for the internal government of the cummunity, in conformity with the laws of the Republic, and shall submit these to the approbation of the Congress, or the Supreme Executive Power.

10. The articles which said settlers may ship in the ports of the Republic shall be free from all export duty during a period of eight years.

These concessions shall in no manner operate to the prejndice of the projected Inter-Oceanic Railroad; for, whatever privileges have been, or may hereafter be granted to the latter, shall be an exception to the present concessions.

Let it be understood: that the privileges before mentioned relative to the establishment of machines, shall be confined to the departments of Santa Barbara, Gracies and Comayagua; excepting for the machine for manufacturing cloths, which shall extend to the whole Republic.

If within three years the number of persons in the city now to be founded does not ascend to five hundred at least, the privileges granted under this Act shall remain without effect; but, in such case the immigrants who may already be established shall have the right of property to such portions of the land granted as shall be found under cultivation.

Written in Comayagua, in the Government House, on the 8th day of May, 1867.—J. Lopez, Ponseano Leiva.

{ SEAL. }

A true copy,
San Pedro, Jan. 29th, 1868.
J. REYNAUD.

9

On the 22d of April 1867 the Act given below was passed by the town of San Pedro for the protection of Foreign Immigrants.

Acta Municipal de las Autoridades de San Pedro, protejiendo a los Inmigrantes Estrangeros.

JOSE MARIA MERLO,

Secretario de la Municipalidad de San Pedro,

Certifico: que en el libro de actas y acuerdos que la Municipalidad lleva en el corriente año, se encuentra el acuerdo que literalmente dice: "Sala de Sesiones Municipales, San Pedro, Abril veinte y dos de mil ochocientos sesenta y siete.

La Municipalidad de San Pedro, reunida estraordinariamente en union del Consejo y otros vecinos, presidida por el señor Alcalde Municipal. En seguida, despues de oida la solicitud expuesta por el coronel Mr. Green Malcolm, natural de los Estados Unidos de Norte America, representante de la emigracion de dichos Estados, que hoy ha arribado y que arribe en lo sucesivo a esta poblacion con animo de avecindarse; por si y a nombre de sus consosios, pidio se les conceda poblarse con nosotros, y terrenos de los nuestros para edificar casas, para habitaciones, para maquinas, fabricas o manufacturas de coser, tejer, aserrar y otras, y para cultivar. La Municipalidad, considerando: 1o. Que el territorio de la Republica de Honduras es un asilo para todo estrangero, maxime que venga a trabajar de cualquier manera en el. 2o. Que ofreciendo Mr. Malcolm por si y sus consocios establecer fabricas y manufacturas en el pais; y ademas, enseñar a los hijos de este mismo, dichos oficios u otros. 3o. Establecer una ruta de comunicacion por el Chamaleco entre Omoa y San Pedro para exportar é importar mercancias suyas y de los del pais, cobrandoles a estos precios equitativos tanto, que les cueste dos o tres veces ménos que el alquiler de una mula por el transporte. 4o. Vivir fraternalmente con los de este pais y servirse mutuamente. 5o. Acatar las autoridades, las leyes y la religion del pais, y contribuir por su parte al respeto, observancia y cumplimiento de las primeras, de modo, que si entre ellos alguno faltare a su dicho respeto y observancia, pediran y haran que sea castigado segun las mismas leyes. 6o. Y establecer colejios y escuelas de enseñanza para sus hijos y los de este pais, cuando se radiquen. Y la Municipalidad en consecuencia, oyendo al consejo, acordo. 1o. Dar a todo estrangero que quiera radicarse en San Pedro, derecho en los ejidos de esta poblacion para edificar casas para habitacion, para maquinas o fabricas de tejer, coser, acerrar maderas y otras que deseen establecer despues, y para el cultivo de caña, algodon, café, etc. 2o. Que los Norte Americanos que hoy han llegado y llegaren a establecerse en San Pedro, no podran impedir a ningun centroamericano, o de otra nacion amiga, que viniere a avecindarse, que quisiere edificar casa cerca de las suyas en los lugares que no tengan occupados. 3o. Que el derecho que tengan en los ejidos sera igual al que tienen los vecinos de San Pedro para cultivar, para cortar maderas, sean o no para construccion, para materiales de sus casas, fincas y de otras cosas para que quieran hacer uso, menos para exportarlas como articulo mercantil. 4o. Igual derecho tendran a las plantas medicinales y frutas silvestres sin dueño, que se encuentren en dichos ejidos para que hagan uso de ellas. Tambien tendran derecho al uso de la madera para leña y de las aguas para sus maquinas, siempre que las necessitaren, si de esto no resultare daño alguno al comun del pueblo. 5o. Que ninguno de los vecinos de San Pedro les molestara ni inquietara por la posesion de lo que adquieran bajo de los principios de esta concesion ; y el que lo hiciere, sera castigado como perturbador de la paz y tranquilidad de las familias. 6o. Que de este acuerdo se le dé testimonio a Mr. Malcolm para que lo presente a S. E. el Sr. Presidente de la Republica, para que si lo estimase por conveniente, se sirva darle su soberana aprobacion, o que disponga lo que fuere mas conforme. Asi se acordo, firmando la Municipalidad, el Consejo y vecinos que concurrieron por ante mi el presente Secretario que doy fé, Monico Padilla. Por el Senor Rejidor Don Pablo Caliz, que no sabe firmar, y por mi como Sindico, Antonio Zarabia. Por los Consejeros Don Juan Zuniga. Don Juan Caliz y Don Luis Matamoros que no saben firmar, y por mi como Consejero, Manuel Cruz. Timoteo Quintera. Lazaro Bardales, por mi padre Serapio Reyes, que no sabe firmar y por los Senores Don Jorge Vallecillo, y Don Concepcion Vallecillo. Andres Reyes. Manuel Caliz. José Reynaud. Rufino Gonzales. Eduardo Buchmar. José Maria Merlo, Secretario. Concuerda con su orijinal a que remito de donde lo saqué literalmente, a pedimento verbal de Mr. Malcolm, en San Pedro, a los veinte-y-tres dias del mes de Abril de mil ochosientos sesenta-y-siete. José Maria Merlo, Secretario.

Es conforme.

San Pedro, Enero 31, 1868.

J. REYNAUD.

(TRANSLATION.)

A Municipal Act of the Authorities of San Pedro, for the Protection of Foreign Immigrants.

I, Jose Maria Merlo, Secretary of the Municipality of San Pedro, do herby certify :

That in the Book of Acts and Resolutions, of the Municipality for this year, is found the Resolution which literally says :

Municipal Session Hall, San Pedro, April 22, 1867.

The Municipality of San Pedro, in extraordinary session assembled, in conjunction with the Council and other citizens, presided by his Honor the Alcalde Municipal, and after hearing the petition presented by Col. Green Malcolm, a native of the United States of North America, representing the emigration from said States already arrived or that may hereafter arrive at this place, with the object of domiciliating here, for himself and in behalf of his associates, he solicits the right of settling among us, and also the grant of lands to build houses for residence, and for machine-shops and manufactories of various kinds, such as—Clothing manufactories, Saw Mills, etc., and also for agricultural purposes ; Therefore, the Municipality, considering :

1st.—That the territory of the Republic of Honduras offers a home to all foreigners, particularly to the industrious who may wish to settle upon its soil ;

2d. That Mr. Green Malcolm, for himself and in the name of his fellow settlers, offers to establish machines and manufactories in the country, and to teach to the natives of the soil the use and management of the same, and other trades ;

3d. To establish a highway for transit by the Chamlicon, between Omoa and San Pedro, to import and export merchandise for themselves and for the natives, requiring from the latter such reasonable prices as will amount to about one-third the hire of a mule.

4. To live in good harmony with the natives, fraternizing with and helping each other.

5. To respect the authorities, the laws and the religion of the country, and to contribute on their part, to the respect, observance and execution of the same, so that if any of them should fail in this particular, they shall demand and see that he be punished according to the laws.

6. To establish Colleges and Schools for their children and those of the natives.

And the Municipality after hearing the Council did therefore resolve :—

1. To grant to each and every foreigner wishing to settle in San Pedro, the right to build on the public lands of this community, houses of residence, machine-shops and manufactories of various kinds, for cloths and clothing, saw mills, aud such others as they may wish to establish afterwards ; and also for the cultivation of Cotton, Sugar Cane, Coffee, &c.

2. That the North Americans who have arrived or may hereafter arrive here for the purpose of settling in San Pedro, shall not oppose any Central-American, or citizens of any friendly nations who may come to settle, and erect buildings on the unoccupied lands in their vicinity.

3. That their right in relation to public lands shall be the same as those enjoyed by the citizens of San Pedro, for cultivation, for making lumber, whether for building purposes or for the use of their establishments, or other purposes, excepting for exportation as an article of merchandise.

4. They shall have an equal right to the medicinal plants and wild fruits on the public lands ; also the right to cut wood for

fuel, and to the use of the water for their machines, whenever they may need them, provided no prejudice result therefrom to the public at large.

5th. That no citizen of San Pedro shall molest or disturb them in the possession of whatever they may acquire under this Act: and any one so doing, shall be punished as a disturber of the peace and tranquility of the community.

6th. That this Act be communicated to Mr. Malcolm, that he may present it to His Excellency the President of the Republic, in order that, should he deem it expedient, he may give it his sovereign approval, or otherwise dispose as he may think proper.

Thus agreed, and signed by the Municipality, the Council and citizens who concurred, before me, the present Secretary, to which I hereby certify.—Monico Pedilla, by the Señor Regidor Don Pablo Cadiz, who cannot sign his name, and by me as Syndic, Antonio Zarabia; for the Councilmen Don Juan Zuniga, Don Juan Cadiz, and Don Luis Matamoros, who cannot write, and for myself Manuel Cruz. Timoteo Quintero, Lazaro Bardalis. Por mi padre, Seraphio Reyes, who cannot sign, and for Messrs. Jorge Vallecillo and Concepcion Vallecillo,—Andres Reyes. Manuel Cadiz, José Reynaud—Rufino Gonzalez—Eduardo Buckmar. José Maria Merlo, Secretario: This agrees with the original from which I copied it literally, at the verbal request of Mr. Malcolm, in San Pedro, on the 23d day of the month of April, 1867. — José Maria Merlo, Secretary.

A true copy:

San Pedro, January 31, 1868.

J. REYNAUD.

The following is from the Legislative Bulletin of March 14th, 1866 :

El Presidente de la Republica de Honduras a sus Habitantes :

Sabed : Que el Soberano Congreso ha decretado lo siguiente :

" El Soberano Congreso con el fin de establecer las condiciones bajo las cuales debe admitirse en la Republica la inmigracion estrangera ; y en complimento del articulo 19 de la Constitucion, ha tenido a bien

DECRETAR.

ARTICULO 1o. Se concede a todos los estrangeros que quieran domiciliarse en Honduras, los derechos que gocen los nativos con areglo a las leyes, a las cuales quedaran sugetos los inmigrantes, desde el momento en que adquieran vecindario.

ART. 2o. El estrangero que desde el dia en que obtenga carta de vecindad, en cinco anos, cultive positivamente un terreno nacional, estableciendo en el, fincas estables, lo hara suyo en propriedad, pudiendo sacar de otros terrenos nacionales contiguos, los aprovechamientos necesarios para su finca.

ART. 3o. Los estrangeros gosaran el privilegio de no prestar servicios militares en un periodo de diez años, salvo el caso de guerra nacional para repeler una invasion ; y por cuatro años no seran molestados para ningun oficio o empleo concejil.

ART. 4o. Los inmigrantes que profesen otra religion que no sea la dominante, pueden ejercer privadamente su propio culto, y erijir cementerios para sepultar sus cadaveres.

ART. 5o. Los inmigrantes no estaran sujetos, durante ocho años, a tasas ni impuestos extraordinarios ; ni pagaran derechos fiscales por la introduccion de maquinas herramientas, instrumentos y libros para ejercer sus ciencias é industrias.

ART. 6o. El Poder ejecutivo concedera privilegios esclusivos a los estrangeros inventores o introductores de maquinas o procedimientos utiles, no usados en el pais.

ART. 7o. En todo tiempo, los estrangeros libres de responsabilidad legal, podran emigrar y disponer de sus intereses a su arbitrio.

ART. 8o. A los inmigrantes que tomen en arrendamiento, tierras o fincas de propriedad particular, no se les cobrara mas canon o pension, que la que por costumbre se haya exijido a los nativos.

ART. 9o. Las concesiones de esta ley se entienden acordadas tambien, a favor de los inmigrantes de las Republicas de America,

Dado en el Salon de sesiones del Congreso Nacional. Comaayagua, Febrero 26 de 1866. Juan Lopez, D. P. Carlos Madrid, D. S. Jeronimo Zelaya, D. S.

Es conforme a su original.

San Pedro, Febrero 3 de 1868.

J. REYNAUD.

TRANSLATION.

COMAYAGUA, 14th March, 1866.

The President of the Republic of Honduras,

To its Inhabitants :

Be it known : That the Sovereign Congress has decreed the following :

" The Sovereign Congress, with the view of laying down the conditions under which Foreign Immigration is to be admitted into the Republic ; and in complianc with article 19 of the Constitution, hereby

DECREES :

ART. 1. To all foreigners wishing to domiciliate in Honduras are granted the rights enjoyed by the Natives under the laws, to which Immigrants shall be subject from the moment they acquire a domicil.

ART. 2, The foreigner who, within five years from the day he obtains his certificate of residence, shall positively cultivate some national land, establishing thereon permanent farms, will thereby acquire the right of property to said land, and shall moreover have the right of taking from other contiguous Government lands such materials as may be necessary for the improvement of his place.

ART. 3. Foreigners shall enjoy the privilege of exemption from military service during a period of ten years, except in case of national war to repel invasion; and during four years shall not be required to perform any civil duty.

ART. 4. Immigrants whose religious creed may be different from the prevailing religion, may privately follow their own religion and erect cemeteries for the dead.

ART. 5. Immigrants shall not be subject, during eight years, to any tax or impost, nor have to pay fiscal duties for the introduction of machinery, tools, instruments and books for the use of their professional or industrial pursuits.

ART. 6. The Executive Power shall grant exclusive privileges to foreigners who may invent or introduce machines, or useful improvements, not in use in this country.

ART. 7. At all times, foreigners free from all legal responsibility shall be at liberty to imigrate and to dispose of their interests at their own will.

ART. 8. Immigrants who may take on lease private lands, or farms, shall not be required to pay higher contributions than is usually required from natives.

ART. 9. The benefits granted under this law are understood to extend also to immigrants from the Republics of America.

Given in the Session Hall of the National Congress. Comayagua, February 26, 1866. Juan Lopez, D. P.—Carlos Madrid, D. S.—Jeronimo Zelaya, D. S.

A true copy :

San Pedro, February 3, 1868.

J. REYNAUD.

Knowing that the Official Gazette of all countries is supposed to reflect the sentiment of the Government, the following is inserted to give information that may be of value, or at least of interest to those who contemplate removing to Spanish Honduras.

(*Copia.*)

(Parrafo tomado del Tomo 6o, Numero 73, de la Gaceta Oficial de Honduras.)

EMIGRADOS CULTIVADORES Y EMIGRADOS POLITICOS.

" Nuestra industria y nuestra civilizacion que tanto reclaman el advenimiento de estrangeros pacificos con designios de radicarse en el pais, comienzan a recibir beneficios de la emigracion de cultivadores, que andando el tiempo daran a nuestras riquezas naturales todo el valor que merecen y que hoy se desconoce."

" Ha venido a las costas de Omoa un numero considerable de familias de los Estados Unidos con capitales y herramientas ; se estan haciendo plantaciones que bastante prometen, y se espera el continuado ingreso de otras familias. Mientras tanto, se inician algunas contratas para la ejecucion del proyectado Ferrocarril Inter-Oceanico, que como por encanto cambiara, cuando se verifique, la suerte de este pais estacionado y comprimido entre dos mares por falta de una via ferrea que los comunique."

" La Republica pues, pasados sus recientes quebrantos por la guerra de Olancho, toca una época en que comenzaran a desarrollarse sus incalculables elementos de prosperidad, bajo los auspicios de la paz y de la nueva legislacion que hoy rije."

" Aparte de las contratas que sancione el proximo Congreso, hay una ley bastante liberal para atraer la inmigracion estrangera, y el Poder Ejecutivo esta facultado para aumentar las concesiones. En efecto, hay la mejor disposicion para que asi se realice; pero con tan prudentes reservas, que en ningun caso puedan convertirse en amenazas o peligros para la nacion, los bienes que se dispensen al elemento civilizador que pretende favorecernos."

" Por lo mismo cumple al buen sentido con que ira procediendose en esta parte, que sea bien conocida de todos la politica del mismo Gobierno."

" No es aceptable en sus determinaciones, el hecho de que se establescan colonias que asuman la aptitud de grupos en que prevalezca la solaridad de un estrangerismo peligroso."

" Tampoco seran aceptables los derechos esclusivos en favor de algunas naciones, gremios o individuos, que impidan a otros los comunes beneficios que las leyes del pais ofrecen a todos los emigrados pacificos del mundo."

" En lo concerniente a la via ferrea, sera preferible el proyecto que en mejores terminos brinde mas garantias de practicabilidad."

" En orden a emigrados politicos de las vecinas Republicas, el Gobierno muy interesado en la paz de Centro-America, cumplira con fidelidad los tratados que sobre la materia existen con algunas de ellas; y respecto de las que no medien pactos expresos, hara que inflexiblemente se observe con sus respectivos emigrados lo que el Derecho de Gentes previene, sin permitirles que ejerzan hostilidades contra sus gobiernos ; pero esto de tal modo, que en casos indefinidos, no se infrinja la Constitucion de la Republica, por que el Presidente de ella esta dispuesto a sostener á todo trance ese codigo que le cupo en honra sancionar sin serle dable hollarlo, por que en eso seria una inconsecuencia culpable."

Es conforme.

SAN PEDRO, FEBRERO 11, 1868.

J. REYNAUD.

TRANSLATION.

(Extract from the 6th Volume, No. 73, of the "Gazeta Oficial" of Honduras.)

"AGRICULTURAL EMIGRANTS AND POLITICAL EMIGRANTS.

"Our industry and civilization, so much in need of energetic, experienced and enterprising men, already begin to give unmistakable evidences of the immense benefits to be derived by our country from the advent and permanent settlement on our soil of the industrious and enlightened immigrants whom the liberal policy of our Government is now attracting to our shores, and whose labors, we have no doubt, will soon soon render available the hitherto hidden and unprofitable treasures of our fertile soil.

"A considerable number of immigrants provided with capital and agricultural implements have already arrived from the United States, and the various plantations which here and there have sprung up under their care, promising a just reward for their labors, cannot fail to insure the continued influx of this desirable class of population. At the same time several contracts are on foot for the building of the projected Interoceanic Railroad, which will, when realized, change, as if by enchantment, the fate of this country now bound and compressed between two seas, for want of a railroad to establisl communication between them.

"The Republic, then, free from the recent troubles of the wa of Olancho, has now reached a period when, under the auspice of peace and a wise legislation, the incalculable resources of it soil will begin to develop.

"Apart from the contracts which will be sanctioned by th next Congress, there is a law sufficiently liberal to attract fo eign Immigration, and the Executive Power is authorized t increase the concessions. In fact, the law contains the be dispositions for the realization of this object; but under suc prudent restrictions, that in no case, can the benefits and priv leges thus conferred, be converted into a dangerous power our midst.

"It is therefore important for all parties to understand t true policy of the Government on this subject.

"It is not in the spirit of that policy to tolerate the tablishment of colonies that would assume the attitude groups in which would prevail the solidarity of a danger foreignism.

"Neither should it be interpreted as granting rights or pr leges to certain nations, corporations or individuals, that wo exclude others from the common benefits which the laws of country offer to all peaceable immigrants from all parts of world.

"In relation to the Railroad, that plan will be most accept that shall give the best guarantee of practicability.

"With regard to political emigrants from the neighbo Republics, the Government, much interested in the p of Central America, will faithfully conform with the tre which exist between some of them and this Government; and with respect to emigrants from those republics with whom we have as yet no treaty, they shall be dealt with according to the strictest principles of reason and equity; not permitting them in any case to exercise hostilities against their own government; but this, in such manner, that in cases not defined, the Constitution of the Republic shall not be infringed, for the President is determined to enforec at all times the provisions of that Instrument which he had the honor of sanctioning, without being at liberty to violate it.

A true copy:

San Pedro, February 11, 1868.

J. REYNAUD.

The Council elected in 1867 continued in office till the 18th of February, 1868, when a new Council was elected, the following gentlemen being chosen; Dr. G. P. Frierson the Presiding officer.

Dr. G. P. Frierson,	D. P. Ferguson,
W. B. Tindle, Sr.,	L. G. Pirkle,
G. A. Haralson,	A. J. Hill, Secry.

In consequence of a difference of opinion existing between the authorities of San Pedro and Maj. Malcolm concerning the Mayor's authority over, and right to grant titles to the town lands as Agent of the Bureau of Emigration, the matter was put to rest by the Major signing the following paper, which was made a matter of public record.

(*Copy.*)

"As I do not wish to be misunderstood or misrepresented, I hereby repeat what I have stated to Dr. Frierson and others at different times, that any one desiring to settle on the District of land called Medina, and which was conceded by the town of San Pedro in an official Act dated April 22, 1867, to settlers, have the ability, with my consent, to choose their location and 150 acres to a man of family and 100 acres to a single man, and that they have the right to apply to the authorities of San Pedro for titles or rely upon my obtaining titles for them as they may choose. That I make no objection to any settler except on account of unworthiness to be established by me. The cost to be at the expense of each settler, unless the General Government decide that titles are only to be made by the authorities of San Pedro; and in that case, I obligate myself to refund all such costs made to me. In the event that the General Government decide that titles to said lands shall be made through other channels, then I obligate myself to furnish indisputable titles, without additional costs, and in whatever manner the Government may direct. Having promised as a citizen of the country and as an officer of Government, to be controlled in all things by my superiors.

February 24, 1868.

(*Signed*) G. MALCOLM.

WITNESSES :

(*Signed*) G. P. Frierson,
" W. J. Walters,
" L. G. Pirkle.

The following notice being found posted, is copied for information.

NOTICE.

At a meeting of the City Council of Medina, February 24, the following resolution was passed :

That any one wishing a lot in Medina, can obtain the same by paying register fee, (one dollar) with the privilege of buying an additional lot for the sum of 25 dollars; provided the first lot be cleared off immediately and improved within six months; the second to be cleared and improved within twelve months. A house to be erected on one of the lots within six months. The above privilege to close on June first.

February 26, 1868.

(*Signed*) G. P. FRIERSON,
Chairman.

SAN PEDRO SULA.

The town of San Pedro is situated on the plain of Sula, in the department of Santa Barbara, and is about thirty miles from Omoa, though the natives state the distance to be about fifty miles. An *attempt* has been made to describe the routs to it, and we will now give a short account of the town and its surroundings. The town is certainly most delightfully situated, two and a half miles from the mountains on the west, whose tops are frequently enveloped in clouds, and the varying hues of the vegetation on their slopes as the sun rises and descends make a scene that is constantly changing, and which is as pleasing as it is lovely. There are no cisterns or wells, the supply of water being brought from the *Rio de las Piedras*, two and a half miles distant, and passes through the place by four little streams, through which it gurgles over pebbly bottoms, entirely shaded till it reaches the corporate limits of the place. pure, clear and cool from the mountains,

By a regulation of the town the water is not permitted to be disturbed above a certain point, where the supply is obtained for culinary purposes and for drinking. The *Cavildo* (Court house) is constructed of large sun dried bricks, or adobes, and is covered with tile, as is also the church edifice and several other houses in the place, but most of the buildings have mud walls and are covered with branches of the Cahoon. Not a chimney is to be seen in the place; not a pane of glass; and only two plank floors. The houses are all one story. The country north, south and east of town is cultivated in patches of from five to fifty acres, where the orange, plantain, banana, pine-apple and other fruits may be found growing. From sun rise till noon it is best to keep in the shade as the heat is oppressive, but after that time we have never known a breeze to fail to spring up from the north, which prevails with greater or less force till sun-set. It is a somewhat remarkable fact that when the thermometer indicates 70°., the temperature. judging from the feelings, seems to be at least 10°. lower. The least that can be said is, this is a lovely spot, but the means of getting to it, and other objections that seem insurmountable, should, if possible, be removed. Population from 500 to 600; 200 of which are emigrants, and the remainder mixed.

The productions of both Spanish Honduras and British Honduras are very much the same with the exception of cacao and coffee, both of which seem to us better here than in British Honduras. Mahogany, fustic, log-wood, rose-wood, and other woods of value are alike common in both countries, as is also the caoutchouc, or India-rubber. Most of the wood of both Spanish Honduras and British Honduras will not split, and the fencing is usually made of logs, or the "Pimente." The following we were told would split, though we saw no rails in the country cedar, one kind of mahogany, laurel, jabon, pine, (which grow on the mountains) and one kind of oak (we saw only the liv oak.) Much of the timber is liable to be attacked by worm and is unsuited to building purposes. The following being used for houses; cedar, mahogany, black laurel, frijolea, oak, cabra-hatcha, and the mother of cacao; the last being very fine for posts, as it is said to be as durable as our locust. The *Motaté*, a hedge plant, is used very extensively, (which we do not remember to have mentioned) which grows to the height of six to eight feet, and resembles the tuft which grows on the top of the pine apple, with briers on each edge, and is impenetrable.

FRUITS.

It is a mistaken idea that fruits of most kinds can be had at all seasons of the year, and that they are superior to the same kinds imported into the United States. The banana and plantain are always to be had, as is also the orange, in some sections, but they *are not* superior in flavor to the same fruits, imported, as it is necessary to gather them, except the orange, in an unripe state, even here, to prevent their destruction by birds. The pine apple is perhaps superior in flavor when left to ripen on the plant, that being the opinion expressed by many, though we could discover but little, if any difference. There are no peaches no pears, no apples and we hardly think any one would exchange those fruits for all that are raised in Honduras. There are two fibrous plants that are worthy of mention, which are extensively used by the natives though comparatively little is prepared for export. The "*Pete*," or silk grass; and the "*Mascal*." From the first fish lines and hammocks are made, and from the second, cordage. The fibre is almost precisely like the manilla, being equally strong, and is prepared without "water rotting." These plants so closely resemble the "*Motaté*" in appearance that they are often mistaken for it.

GAME.

In British Honduras but little game was seen, but in Spanish

Honduras can be found the deer, turkey, a species of grouse, and the *Qualm* which is a bird not unlike the pea fowl, but a little smaller ; also rabbits, quails and pigeons.

FISH.

While the waters of the sea furnish fish in abundance and in great variety, they were not found to be plentiful in the streams in either country we visited.

DUTIES.

The Import duty is 40 per cent on all things but liquor, that being 30 per cent ; 10 per cent of the 40 per cent has to be paid in coin, and 30 per cent in Government paper, which reduces it to about 15 per cent in coin. On liquor, 20 per cent has to be paid in coin, and the balance in Government paper.

Export duty 6 per cent. There is no duty on anything brought into the country by emigrants for their own use.

Exports and Imports.

The annual exports are about as follows : Imports being about the same as exports in amount.

Exports.—	Mahogany, and other woods...........	$300,00(
"	Bullion............................	250,00(
"	Cattle.............................	150,00(
"	Indigo, sugar, hides, tobacco and sarsaparilla.........................	250,00(
	Total.................	$950,00(

REVENUES.

The revenues of the country amount to about $300,000, a large portion of which is derived from the sale of *Aguardiente* (native rum) and tobacco, both of which are Government monopolies.

Most of the money in circulation is the *Macaco* or cut money though there is now considerable American coin to be seen, which passes for its full value, except the dime and half dime.

The Government is popular and representative and composed of three distinct powers, viz: Legislative, Executive, and Judicial. The first residing in the General Assembly, the second in the President, and the third in the Courts.

The religion is the *Roman Catholic to the exclusion of all others*. The following being an extract from the Constitution of the country on that subject.

CAPITULO 3°.

DEL GOBIERNO Y DE LA RELIGION.

ART. 7°.—El Gobierno de la Republica es popular representativo; y se ejercera por tres Poderes distintos: Legislativo, Ejecutivo y Judicial.

ART. 8°.—La Religion de la Republica es la Cristiana, Catholica, Apostolica Roman, con exclusion del ejercicio publico de cualquiera otra. El Gobierno la protege; pero ni este ni autoridad alguna tendran intervencion en el ejercicio privado de las otras que se establezcan en el pais, si estas no tienden a deprimir la dominante y a alterar el orden publico.

Persons born in the state, or any state of Central America are recognized as citizens. Foreigners may acquire the right by act of the Legislature, but as soon as they declare their intention to become citizens are entitled to the protection of citizens.

All citizens over the age of 21 are entitled to vote, but after the year 1870 only those who can read and write will be entitled to that privilege. Any one convicted of a crime is deprived of the right of suffrage. Foreigners become naturalized by marrying in the state, or by holding a given amount of property.

LABORERS AND SERVANTS.

The price usually paid for men, field hands, is from five to seven dollars per month and their provision, and from eight to ten when they feed themselves. For a cook woman, $3 00 per month. For washing (family of four) $2 00 per month—washing not done on the premises ; for a girl 12 years of age, from $1 00 to $1 50 per month ; and for boys of the same age $3 00 per month. As is the case in British Honduras, laborers and servants *are scarce*, and the few to be found are seldom anxious to hire. We do not know of a family of emigrants at San Pedro provided with native servants, they doing their work in most cases themselves ; though there may be some.

DOMESTIC ARRANGEMENTS.

We have said there is not a chimney at San Pedro ; this is the case also in British Honduras except in the towns. The contrivance for cooking is a platform raised about two feet, on which clay to the depth of six inches is placed, and at one side, or rather edge, several little horse-shoe or semi-circular fire places are made on which to place the cooking vessels. It is astonishing to see how small a quantity of wood is necessary to cook a meal by this arrangement. A lady who has lived here for several years informed me she preferred these fire places to a cook stove. Such a thing as a bucket is not to be seen ; porous earthen jars being used instead, the constant evaporation from the surface of which reduces the temperature of the water several degrees. On the table, earthen bottles of a similar material are used instead of pitchers. The women are the most superior washers, yet a wash tub is not used, but what is called a *Battea*, which is a tray, varying in size, but usually two feet and a half in length by one and a half in width. For the benefit of bachelors we will state that they have no use for a wash board, and that only thirty-seven and a half cents per dozen is charged for washing when soap is furnished them, and one dollar if the clothes are starched and ironed. Their work in this line ought to be well done, for our experience (before we commenced doing our own washing) proved that they required one day to wash, one to dry, one to iron, and from one to two more to bring it home, whether it was one piece or a dozen. It seems almost impossible for one person to do anything where two can be employed. In milking, one holds the calabash while another milks with both hands; the calf being tied to a fore leg of the cow.

DOMESTIC ANIMALS.

Neat cattle are plentiful, and can be bought for, from 5 to 10 dollars each, a short distance from San Pedro. Horses and mules are abundant, but very small, and vary in price from 15 to 50 dollars, the latter price being paid for such animals as can be bought with us for the same sum in different funds. The hogs are *very fine* and can be bought low; pork selling for 3 cents per pound. This is no country for sheep, but the goat seems to do very well.

REPTILES AND INSECTS.

We did not see, during our stay in Spanish Honduras, a single snake—though they are said to be numerous. There are some bottle-flies, but not so many as in British Honduras, and in certain localities sand flies are very numerous and annoying. While we saw no mosquitoes at San Pedro, if it is desired to see them in their most gigantic proportions, take a trip on the Chemlicon. During our stay on that river they proved themselves to be the largest, strongest, most persistent in their efforts to annoy, carried the sharpest weapon, and used it more vigorously than any it had ever before been our misfortune to encounter.

Ants are both very large and numerous, and those who succeed in establishing a kitchen garden, and in enjoying the fruit of their labor thus bestowed, consider themselves very fortunate.

OUTFIT FOR HONDURAS.

Having found that we made more than one mistake in this respect, will state that our linen clothing was found not suited to the climate, as we were frequently uncomfortably cool, and it would have been better if thin woolen material had been selected instead. We were induced to purchase "Moccasins" at Belize, and found them to be of little service, though they are worn by men engaged in cutting for export the woods of the country, and by a very large proportion of the natives. If we had provided ourselves with a pair of good boots, it would have been much better. We also found that cotton socks did not answer a good purpose, and it would have been better had we been provided with those made of wool. It is best to have all articles that are to be carried to San Pedro, in packages of one hundred pounds, when it can be done, as two hundred pounds is a load for a mule.

MONEY,

American silver coins, with the exception of dimes and half dimes, pass in both British Honduras and Spanish Honduras, for their full value, and in British Honduras 2½ per cent is allowed for American Gold coin in making purchases, in conformity to law of the country, though it can frequently be sold for 3 or 4 per cent. The English shilling will pass for as much as an American quarter, which fact having been ascertained by us before we left New Orleans, an ample supply of that coin was provided.

OMOA.

The town of Omoa has less than one thousand inhabitants,

and contains no buildings worthy of note, most of the houses being one story, though some are covered with tiles and some with corrugated iron. The system of cleanliness in operation at Belize, is unknown here, and even hogs are slaughtered in the streets.

Commandant of Omoa, ...Gen'l Phil. Espinoza.
American Consul ....Charles Follin.
Belgian and British Consul..................J. F. Debrot.
French Consul,........................—— St. Laurent.

CONCLUSION.

Though it would be pleasant to continue these pages, and give a more detailed account of the fruits, vegetables and minerals of the lands we visited, yet, feeling that we have already written too much to simply convey an idea of the country, must draw to a close. It has been our purpose from beginning to end, to give a fair and candid statement of *facts*, and to endeavor to enable all, *to see as we saw*, feeling satisfied they can draw satisfactory inferences therefrom. Much has been written concerning Honduras, that presented the appearance of speculation, and not unfrequently *by Speculators*, and comparatively little information of a detailed character has been given, which induced us to adopt a plan that we hope will not fail to convey a better idea of the country than has up to this time been attainable without making a trip. This, to the best of our ability, we have endeavored to do, even at the risk of repetition. Whatever may be the pecuniary condition of people, we saw no one in Honduras, who left the United States, whose condition in that respect appeared enviable, and met but one person who had more money than he arrived there with. On the contrary, the emigrant lives in the simplest manner, and we were informed by a gentleman at San Pedro, who was in a position of indepedence once in the States; that for many days his family had not been provided with meat, and that he had no money even to purchase many articles of prime necessity, much less one of luxury—though beef can be bought for three cents per pound and pork at the same price. It is true a very great mistake was made at San Pedro, in planting cotton to the almost entire exclusion of every-thing else, and the crop being destroyed by the Army Worm, and all their means being exhausted, they were compelled through necessity to exercise the most rigid economy. Very few have thus far erected houses, and are now paying for buildings of one room, from 5 to 8 dollars per month.

It has been said of both British and Spanish Honduras, that certain crops can be made of a given quantity, and two crops in a year *without cultivation.* This brings up for consideration the fitness of those countries for agricultural and Horticultural purposes. We have already stated there is much good land to be found, but we saw a much larger proportion than we expected of what seemed very sandy. All seeds and plants must be planted at the commencement of, or during the rainy season which in a great measure prevents cultivation on account of rain if continuous, and we are of the opinion that if cultivation carried to the same extent it was in the States before the war and all grass and weeds removed, the sun will in many localities so parch the soil, that but little will be produced where much may be expected. This is not liable to be the case with sugar cane, rice, the plantain nor banana; the first two covering the ground with a mass of vegetation, and the last two entire shading it around the trees with their broad leaves and there retaining moisture in the earth. It is the custom with t natives to cultivate a piece of ground for one or two years, and then to clear another field, and abandon the first, as it is often easier to clear a new piece than the old, on account of the growth which makes its appearance on a field that has been planted being more difficult to remove. Another reason was given by those who have had experience in cultivating that soil, which was, that in a very few years the soil becomes exhausted to some extent, and it would prove more profitable to change. How will it be with sugar-cane, that (as is the case with all plants containing saccharine matter), draws very heavily on the soil? In Honduras there is no rest for land that is planted in cane, for as soon as a cane is cut another springs up regardless of season, and we would ask, will not this constant and excessive drain soon exhaust one or more constituent elements of the soil, necessary to the growth of the plant? There is no land so rich that it will never become poor, and good cultivators of the soil have always found it to be profitable to rotate crops, and to feed their land before it becomes hungry and to rest it before it became weary. In the United States, vegetation is killed by frost, but in Honduras there is a constant growth of something on the soil, which is greater on land under tendance than on that covered with its primeval growth.

There can be no question that the "Eternal Summer" which prevails in Honduras will be monotonous to a degree that will prove anything but pleasant. To us, autumn has ever been the most interesting season of the year, 'the sere and yellow leaf' indicating a repose of the vegetable kingdom, and never failed to awaken thoughts of a pleasant character, and feelings of reverence. The sighing of the winds of winter through the lattice, the cheerful fireside, with the domestic scene it is unnecessary to describe, make a picture most of us are familiar with, but is lost, forever lost to the emigrant in Honduras, though it can never be forgotten. The beautiful scenery constantly before the eye at San Pedro, must in the course of time lose its novelty, and cease to impress the mind as at first, and draw forth on certain occasions remarks of a similar character to one we heard from a gentleman who had for some time resided in Honduras which was "We can not live on beautiful scenery." What a volume was expressed in these few words, and in the mournful manner in which they were uttered! In conversation with old residents of Belize, they invariably expressed their surprise at persons locating on the coast of that country, which they stated had been attempted from time to time, without profit or health attending the honest and persistent efforts of those who selected that portion of the country. Most of those persons who left this country with the view of making Honduras their future home, did so because of the unsettled condition of affairs at the South, and under belief that any clime would prove better than the one they were leaving, on which point a very great mistake has been made, and we undertake to say without hesitation, that a large number would return at once if they were in possession of sufficient means to enable them to do so. Many on leaving their homes either "swore in their wrath," or affirmed in their agony that they would never return, which will keep them away, whatever obstacles they may be called upon to remove, or privations they may have to endure. We have in our mind's eye several gentlemen of education, great energy, and influence, who are in this position, and will they not succeed in keeping many in the country who if left to exercise their own judgement would leave at an early day? While many are leaving the "land of their birth," because of the character of the Government under which they are living, or we might say the almost entire absence o

Government, would it not be well, first to examine into the character of the Government they are about to remove to? And on the point of social equality, which is to some a hideous phantom, that at times threatens to assume the density of a solid, would it not be well to exercise a little thought before packing up?

In closing, we indulge the hope that if hereafter any should select the countries of Central America in order to benefit their condition, that they need not necessarily undertake the movement without some information that will be more valuable to them than any we were able to obtain before leaving New Orleans. And if we are the means of preventing disappointment or suffering, even to a limited extent, our purpose will be more than accomplished, and our most sanguine expectations realized. While we give no advice, having studiously avoided doing, so, we would regret to hear of persons leaving this country without sufficient means to enable them to return. For to be thrown upon a distant shore, among people with whom we have few thoughts or feelings in common, and to be compelled to remain, if a favorable impression is not made, is a condition we have never experienced, and cannot describe, but which would be anything but pleasant, particularly if women and children should be of the number. Our task is done, and we can honestly say was undertaken more for the purpose of benefiting our fellow citizens than for any other reason, and in accordance with what many friends have been pleased to call the exercise of a Christian duty.

THE END.

PUBLISHED BY

GEORGE ELLIS,

Bookseller and Stationer,

NO. 7 OLD LEVEE ST.,

OPPOSITE POST OFFICE,

NEW ORLEANS.

Copies mailed free of postage, on receipt of price.

www.ingramcontent.com/pod-product-compliance
Lightning Source LLC
LaVergne TN
LVHW021418110826
845150LV00007B/1984

* 9 7 8 1 4 2 5 5 0 9 0 2 6 *